NO
GOOD-BYES

NO
GOOD-BYES

The Mysterious

Disappearance of

the McStay Family

RICK BAKER

TATE PUBLISHING
AND ENTERPRISES, LLC

Published by Tate Publishing & Enterprises, LLC
127 E. Trade Center Terrace | Mustang, Oklahoma 73064 USA
1.888.361.9473 | www.tatepublishing.com

Tate Publishing is committed to excellence in the publishing industry. The company reflects the philosophy established by the founders, based on Psalm 68:11,
"The Lord gave the word and great was the company of those who published it."

Book design copyright © 2013 by Tate Publishing, LLC. All rights reserved.
Cover design by Lauro Talibong
Interior design by Jomel Pepito

Published in the United States of America

ISBN: 978-1-62510-421-2
True Crime / Hoaxes & Deceptions
13.02.05

Dedication

To Gianni and Joseph Mateo, the innocents.

Contents

Preface

According to the National Center for Missing and Exploited Children (NCMEC), an astounding 2,300 Americans are reported missing every day, including both adults and children.

This number includes nearly 800,000 children younger than eighteen. Over 200,000 are abducted by family members, and 58,000 are abducted by non family members.

Reports of missing persons have increased over sixfold in this country in the past thirty years, from roughly 150,000 in 1980 to around 900,000 in 2012. This increase was driven in part by the country's growing population and also that law enforcement treats these cases more seriously now, including those of marginalized citizens. Annual statistics are not kept for entire families that go missing as it is very rare.

According to the NCMEC, statistics on missing families are not kept because it is a rarity for an entire family to disappear.

However, on the evening of February 4, 2010, an entire family of four mysteriously vanished from their Southern California home.

Joseph Mcstay, his wife Summer, and their two children Gianni and Joseph Mateo had disappeared from the face of this planet.

It seems that just about everyone in this country has heard of this family. When I mention I have written a book about a missing family from Southern California, more often than not, the response has been "Oh, you mean the McStays?"

In the past three years, the FBI, Homeland Security, Interpol, the Mexican Federales, as well as numerous National Missing Persons agencies have investigated this disappearance with nothing but dead ends.

Family members and other supporters have launched Facebook pages, some with thousands of likes, in an effort to get the word out about the McStays. Still, three years later, the McStays remain missing.

One day they were living their lives as a normal family, the next day they were gone.

What happened to the McStay family? Did they meet with foul play, as many believe, or did they decide to start a new life somewhere else? Are there four bodies buried in a shallow Southern California grave, or are Joseph and Summer watching all this commotion from afar, smiling as they sip their margaritas?

Introduction

If my brother and his family suddenly vanished, I would do everything in my power to find them.

I would launch a reward fund and beg for donations.

I would relocate to my brother's city so that I could be involved hands-on with the search.

I would put aside all differences I may have with other members in my extended family for the expressed purpose of finding my brother and his family.

I would work tirelessly with law enforcement, offering any assistance I might provide, knowing their resources are limited.

I would be thankful for any and all publicity on the case, hoping someone might see my family. If someone wanted to write a book about the disappearance, I would contribute in every way possible, knowing it may lead a reader to my brother and his family.

I would be at a loss for words if someone offered a large reward for my family out of their personal funds. I would do all I could to publicize this reward.

Chances are that if your brother and his family disappeared, you would do just about the same things I would.

Not so with the McStay family and some of the friends.

In my opinion, Joseph's and Summer's siblings along with some of their friends and business associates have gone to great lengths to keep their family from being found.

When I offered a $25,000 reward for the McStays, I was maligned by all sides of the extended family.

When I spent thousands of dollars of my personal funds searching for the Mcstays, they publicly mocked me.

Instead of supporting a book with the expressed purpose of finding their family, Joseph's and Summer's extended family members resisted, interfered, and altered documents they had put online that might have helped locate the family and even launched a campaign against my publisher. Why? Read on.

Why I Wrote This Book

It appeared to be just another typical Southern California morning in March 2010, but the Café Bravo in downtown Fallbrook was abuzz with conversations about a local family who had recently vanished.

"What do you think happened to them?" said the young mother at the table to my left. "I think they are in witness protection," her friend answered. To my right was a family of four, and the father was obviously concerned about the disappearance. "It doesn't add up," he said to his wife. "Families of four don't just suddenly disappear. Not here anyway." And he would be right.

Fallbrook is a throwback to days gone by in California. This is a very conservative town with a strong sense of community, home to more avocado trees than palm trees, and a place where violent crimes were previously unheard of. A modern day Mayberry if you will.

This was my introduction to the missing McStay family. Joseph, Summer, Gianni, and Joseph Junior, who, on February 4, 2010, mysteriously vanished from their Fallbrook, California, home.

For the next fourteen months, I would follow this unsolved mystery from a distance like most in the country. I watched as family members were interviewed by Geraldo Rivera, Nancy Grace, and Beth Holloway. I read the print articles from *People Magazine*, *USA Today* and the *Los Angeles Times*.

But it wasn't until May of 2011, when I interviewed Joseph's brother, Mike McStay, on my San Diego talk radio program that my attention to this case began to really pique.

Mike's interview was unsettling for me. I believed he was withholding information. He would never look me in the eyes, was very evasive when I asked specific questions, and it seemed to me that he had remade *himself* as the victim in this disappearance instead of his brother and his family.

Following that interview, I was contacted by a number of citizen sleuths around the country who had listened to Mike's interview. They suggested that I speak with Joseph's father, Patrick. In unison, they told me that there was so much more to this disappearance than what had been publicized by law enforcement and that Mike was not telling everything he knew.

By June 2011, I was talking to Patrick almost daily. I learned that he had assembled a team of supporters throughout the country who volunteered their time to help him piece together the events surrounding this mystery. They had tapped the e-mail accounts of Joseph and Summer and had read many of these private messages. They had amassed hundreds of pages of other documents from police reports, from intriguing receipts for purchases the family had made just before they disappeared to possible sightings that had been videotaped. The more I talked to Patrick and these others, the more addicting this mystery became to me.

My conversations with Patrick began to explore the possibility of writing a book to reveal these previously unpublished or little-known-facts about this mystery. Someone had to know something.

By the end of August 2011, I was well on my way to a finished manuscript. I had immersed myself in this mystery that had become a real-life soap opera. When I could convince family members to open up, they would describe in detail the terribly dysfunctional extended family. Friends and business associates of Joseph and Summer told me wild stories about partnerships from hell, thievery, and sexual improprieties.

Then there were the bankruptcies and name changes. Multiple aliases, fake college degrees, fraudulent insurance policies—my head began to spin.

With each interview, I learned there was someone else out there who claimed to have more information: former neighbors who had moved away and claimed to had never been interviewed by law enforcement, a hotel manager who claimed Joseph and Summer stayed at his establishment the night they disappeared, yet had no proof to validate his claim, a friend who says he watched Joseph fill a duffel bag with cash from an unknown safety deposit box, still another friend who says he was with Joseph when he bought a number of "burn phones" at Walmart. While I couldn't prove any of these claims were true, why would these people lie? What did they have to gain?

There was the former friend of Joseph who claims he permitted himself to be hypnotized to recall specific events from over a year ago as if they had just happened. Someone else who claimed to have been with Joseph when he bought a "secret" laptop that has never turned up. Come on, really?

I spent hours inside the McStays' Fallbrook house and came to know it as well as my own, going over every inch of their former home. I must admit, it creeped me out just a bit. I found the "concealed compartment" that a source had told me about, but just like Al Capone's safe, it was empty.

I had promised many of my sources that I would never reveal our conversations, especially to Patrick or any other family member. I gave my word and have kept it, even in presenting this book.

Once I believed I had a manuscript that was worthy of readers, my concern became how this would look to the general public. Would they see Patrick as trying to profit from his son's disappearance? He had already burned his bridges with San Diego County law enforcement and had made many new enemies who would jump at the chance to condemn him over his involvement with this book.

So I established (and funded) the McStay Foundation. Patrick agreed that all of his profits from this book would go directly to this new foundation with its sole mission of finding Joseph and his family and then after to provide funding for family members of other missing persons who were unable to fund any search. It was a moral and lofty undertaking.

However, at this point in my investigation, I had come to believe that Joseph had taken his family voluntarily and fled Fallbrook. It would be much later in this process when my theory would change.

Patrick and I reached an impasse. He believed they were dead. He was certain that if they were alive, they would have contacted him. "They would not put me through this," he would often say to me.

I believed they left on their own and with an agenda.

In the midst of our stalemate, I learned that Patrick had withheld certain documents from me (i.e., e-mails, receipts, phone records, etc.) so as to protect his family and present them as someone they were not and so our professional relationship was at an end. He wanted me to write a book that painted his family as the Brady Bunch and so he kept from me documents that would show otherwise.

Patrick didn't like any of my conclusions and demanded I not publish my book.

Sadly, I was forced to sever all ties with Patrick McStay. I did, however, retain ownership of the manuscript. I had spent hundreds of hours writing and researching and thousands of dollars for travel to interview those with useful information. I had funded the entire process.

Once word was out that I had written a book, no relative of Joseph or Summer would talk to me any longer, and only a few friends would still return my calls. I felt like I had written an unauthorized biography, forced to piece together the McStays' lives without any help from those who knew them best.

Law enforcement was equally unwilling to help. This is the only official statement I ever received:

> The San Diego sheriff's department does not discuss open investigations. Once the case is solved, it is closed or it is submitted to the San Diego District Attorney's Office for consideration. If you have any evidence supporting the reason the McStays disappeared, or their current location, I would appreciate if you could forward that information. Detective Troy DuGal

So in October 2011, I shelved my nearly finished manuscript. I needed a break from the whole sordid affair. I was no longer convinced my book was worth reading now anyway in light of Patrick's undue influence.

The manuscript was still parked on my library shelf when, in the summer of 2012, I was contacted by an investigative group very familiar with the McStay case.

They possessed hundreds of pages of documents related to this case and the family, many unknown except to law enforcement and a select few.

They graciously offered to share this cache of information with me if I would publish my book, with a common goal of finding the family.

A thorough review of these documents convinced me to go forward with rewriting and publishing my

book, with a desired release date of February 4, 2013 —
the three-year anniversary of the disappearance.

The next few months were a whirlwind.

I removed any Patrick McStay influence from the manuscript and rechecked my facts.

I traveled extensively to meet the people who claimed to have seen the family in the past three years. I reviewed surveillance tapes from ferry systems, Walmarts, and Florida restaurants.

I was forced to do all this without any help from Joseph or Summer's siblings, parents, or business associates, who, for some unknown reason, continue to do everything in their power to keep their family from being found.

I am proud of this book and my efforts to seek the truth. While there has been much discussion in the past three years of the known facts in this case, I present information in these pages that has not yet been discussed in any public forum. It is my hope and prayer that this book will be used by the sleuths and amateurs alike as a source of information that will ultimately lead us to answer the consuming question, what happened to the McStays?

Meet the McStay Family

Children are the hands by which we take hold of heaven.

—Henry Ward Beecher

On the surface, Joseph, Summer, Gianni, and Joseph Junior were your typical Southern California family. Living the laid-back Bohemian lifestyle that has attracted so many to move to the Golden State, they were living examples of the American Dream, one of home ownership, self-employment, and a vibrant family. Or were they?

Joseph and Summer moved to Fallbrook from San Clemente, California, just before Thanksgiving 2009. Both of them were licensed real estate agents, and they had been looking for a fixer-upper investment property in the area where they could live for a few years and then sell at a tidy profit.

Such was their Fallbrook house. Located at the end of a quiet cul-de-sac on a street called Avocado Vista Lane, this was a home that was perfect for their family as well as their remodeling skills.

Joseph was excited about the house. Here's what he said in an e-mail to a friend in October 2009:

> Good talkin to you.... My bus, TG has been great! We just bought a 3000 sq.ft house at base of a mountain w/ avocado trees....5 bed 3 bath...loft/game room & big yard for kids to go crazy.... Got a smokin deal at 316K.... It's at the end of 76 & 15... Love it... Since we got it so cheap, we're gonna fix it up more... granite countertops, ss appliances, wood floors ,etc... then sell it in 2 yrs, load up container... And Move Next Store To My Bro ...Harold in KAUIA!!!
>
> Joseph

He told his father something similar about the same time: "I think we can fix this up and sell it in a couple of years, make money, and then move back to the beach so I am closer to the waves."

Summer, however, was against the move from the start, as we will later learn.

At the time of their disappearance, they had already remodeled the bathrooms and kitchen, were in the process of painting the home's interior, and were ready to install the new wood flooring that had just been delivered.

Both Joseph and Summer were self-employed. Joseph was the owner of Earth Inspired Products, a company he founded in the early 2000s.

Joseph would design and install one-of-a-kind water fountains at resorts and multimillion-dollar homes throughout the United States. His creations can be found at the headquarters for Paul Mitchell salons and Hershey's Chocolate, five-star hotels, and many high-end restaurants.

One of his favorites was a magnificent waterfall in a private estate that was thirty feet tall and only four feet wide. Just before he disappeared, he had sold two of his creations to businesses in Saudi Arabia for over $81,000.

Summer was a real estate agent and was apparently just beginning to canvas their new neighborhood in search of prospects and clients. She had ordered her fliers for this endeavor the week before her disappearance.

We would later learn, however, that Summer had been involved in the questionable loan modification mortgage industry and that some of her associates had been indicted for fraud, one just a few days before her disappearance.

Summer often told family and friends how much she cherished the freedom her real estate business gave her. She loved the ability to be a stay-at-home mom for Gianni and Joseph Junior.

Friends and family members are convinced that Joseph loved all his children. All one has to do is spend a short time on Joseph's YouTube channel (http://www.youtube.com/user/jbmcstay) to confirm this. Joseph had posted numerous videos, all involving either their boys or the other "four-legged kids" in their family: Bear, their 170-pound mixed-breed Shepherd, and Digger, their four-month-old rescued puppy.

It appears, on the surface at least, that Summer also loved her children. However, the deeper I dug into the life and past of Summer, the more questions I have about her "motherhood."

Gianni was born on July 9, 2005, and was hard to miss with his bright eyes and long curls. Little Joseph or "Chubba," as his dad liked to call him, was born on January 31, 2007, and was always full of joy and loved to dance. He was the little clown in the family with the infectious smile. These were boys with no cares in the world.

One of the YouTube videos posted shows the boys in dance mode. Little Joseph is dancing in his diapers and pajamas, pointing at the stereo when the song ends and begging, "Pwease, pwease!" In the background is Gianni, dancing around his toy train set and singing along. In the background and behind the cameras is dad Joseph, narrating and laughing as his sons take in the tunes.

My personal video favorite is titled "Bear-Dig," and it was posted January 23, 2010, just eleven days before they would disappear. It's a touching clip of the two four-legged kids and Summer playing after Digger had recently been introduced to the family. Eight-year-old Bear doesn't seem very happy with the family's new addition but is taking it in stride. At the end of the video, Summer is seen leaning over Bear, hugging and kissing him.

These videos are excellent examples of how the McStay family lived their lives—at least on the surface—by simply enjoying one another.

I believe Joseph described his priorities best in his profile on his YouTube account when he wrote, "God, my wife and kids, surf, soccer, and all the beauty in this world make me who I am."

Joseph and Summer confirmed the old adage that "opposites attract."

Joseph was the laid-back surfer type who got along with everyone. He would do almost anything to avoid any kind of confrontation, at times to a fault.

Summer was a bit more aggressive. She wouldn't hesitate to tell you how she felt and would rarely back down once she was engaged. She could be crass one minute and kind the next. I am reminded of one exchange in particular. She was writing to a family member and was angry, to say the least. While one paragraph was laced with profanity of the worst type, in the very next she would write, "I love you, see you soon." One close friend described her as "a Mrs. Dr. Jekyll and Mr. Hyde."

While the McStay marriage might have seemed healthy on the surface, in reality, it was a runaway passenger train about to run out of tracks.

A Crash-and-Burn Marriage

Yeah, I knew Summer, but I was concerned for Joseph in the beginning 'cause I didn't know her so well. She was kind of a free spirit, but a very cunning side too. I used to always call her out but never thought she'd go so far. But seems both her and Joseph kept best behavior in front of me cause I could always tell them 'I told you so' when the marriage didn't work. I used to hassle them about pacing their relationship. Of course they laughed at me back then and already had two kids before even getting married.

—Joseph's friend

Joseph and Summer's marriage was the second for both. While Summer's ended in 1994 and she'd had no contact with her first husband in years, Joseph's first marriage produced a son, who is today sixteen years old. This marriage ended in a divorce in 2002, but the dynamics of this failed marriage would continue to haunt Joseph and Summer right up to the day they disappeared eight years later.

Most family members believe that Joseph's relationship with his son from his prior marriage was strong. While family and friends will cite this father-son bond as proof that he never left voluntarily, I don't believe this.

Joseph loved his son deeply, but his parenting time and daily involvement with him was diminishing. I believe this was because Summer was jealous and didn't support Joseph's relationship with his son.

On the surface, Summer supported Joseph's firstborn, but when her husband's back was turned, she was actually working to end any relationship Joseph would have with his son going forward.

Consider this e-mail that Summer sent to her sister in the fall of 2005. It reveals Summer's jealousy for Joseph's firstborn and to what lengths she will go to break the bond of the father-son relationship:

> Well, now that I said I'm leaving he has had a change of heart and is begging me not to leave. Agreeing with me that it was wrong of them to expect me to take him whenever they wanted/ needed without consulting me first.

> I also told him that the visitation agreement has to be revised since it was created when they were both single and now they each have new partners and babies to consider.

> We already have him 4 days out of the week ending in every weekend and I can't be relied

on to take care of him when he's working. What did he do when I wasn't here? Why doesn't her new husband watch him?

Why is it that I've only spoken maybe three times to her and she doesn't have the common sense to call me and make sure I'm ok with watching her son, knowing that I've already said No? Mentioning that not once has she ever thanked me for watching her son, when in fact I am still only his girlfriend that he got knocked up?

She does not know me from Adam. Why would either one of them assume that it is okay to leave their son with someone who is not interested in babysitting on that particular day? If they actually cared the way they claim they would never force their kid on someone.

I went on to explain that I'm happy to help him co-parent when he is here because I love children and he is damn lucky that I'm not the sort to be abusive and mean when he is not around like so many other people do when they don't want to be bothered with some else's child.

But ultimately it is his responsibility, not mine. I told him that her new husband must feel the same way because he never takes him either. The new spouses are the CO-Parents not the Real-Parents, which have the full responsibility. Just because we're together she can't see me as her new babysitter because I refuse to take that job.

I would never expect that of my ex's girlfriend would be okay with watching my son. In fact I would go out of my way to make sure everything was all right before I sent my son over. Communication is something that would be high on my list.

Why hasn't she phoned me to ask if he was okay or speak with him? She never calls and checks on him whenever he's away and as a matter of fact nor does SD, which is wrong of both of them. They both are assuming a lot and lying to themselves about how great they are as parents. How can you go four days and not call to see how your eight yr. old son is doing or speaking to the babysitter?

If she can't even call me to check on her son, how is it that she can assume I will watch him? Which goes for SD as well. He was actually very good about listening to me but only after he tried to be all tough and I told him to shove it all up his ass.

I went on to explain we had better work this out tonight or not at all, I can only afford one day of sadness and frustration.

I'm growing a baby that I want to feel loved with or without him.

He and & I have no binding contract so KNOW IT! Otherwise, I'm leaving tomorrow with all my s*** & animals.

I'd call when Baby "G" is born. Suddenly, he had a change of heart. I couldn't really sleep with the baby moving all night and lots of cramps. I feel drained and I'm sure he feels like s*** too. He went to bed with tears in his eyes. I guess we're all having growing pains. I felt very sad about all of this esp. for Baby "G"

But I also know it wouldn't work if I kept quite, at the very least I should explain why I'm leaving.

As all of this is happening the phone rings and its an Agent with a possible Buyer for my house. Life is so STRANGE!!! Our friend Mcgyver was visiting earlier before SD got home and he said that Praylay & SD should not see me as the babysitter either, it was cool that he said it on his own when he discovered that I was watching him during the week and was trying to make birth arraignments.

He's the one bringing me books from the Newport Beach Library and was over to check on me. He may also have a hotel hook up for us. So, now you know the rest of our s**t and doesn't it feel good to be free and single? Yes, sisteroooo life is a bitch but better life than you.

Hope your having lots of fun despite all my drama. Wish you were here for a big hug. Miss you much.

Loves, Me & Baby G.

It does something to the soul of a father when he is forced to choose between his children from two separate families. Summer was making him choose. She was giving him an ultimatum: "Either you back off from your firstborn, or I'm leaving tomorrow, taking all my stuff and animals, and will call you when Baby G is born."

Nothing positive ever comes from a second marriage where one spouse interferes with the parent's relationship with children from the first marriage.

In the next few years, Summer would do everything in her power to end Joseph's relationship with his firstborn. However, this apparently was not enough for Summer. I believe she was hatching a plan that would level false abuse charges against Joseph's firstborn in hopes of ending any relationship between the two. These false allegations would be leveled in 2009 and would also involve the boy's stepfather. This was an incurable miscalculation on her part.

Now fast-forward two years to September 2007 and an e-mail that Summer had sent Joseph. She had learned that he was searching for her biological father, possibly to invite him to their wedding, which would take place in two months on November 10. Here is the text from their wedding invitation:

> As unique as a seashell, as deep as the sea, as eternal as the waves, our love is meant to be. It is with joy that we, Summer Martelli and Joseph McStay, invite you to share in our happiness on Saturday, the 10 of November, two thousand

and seven, at four pm at Rancho Capistrano San Juan Capistrano, California.

A very touching invitation written by Summer herself. Now read the following e-mail, also written by Summer:

> Hey, I just finished a long conversation with my MOM. She had a lot to say so I have to get this thru your BIG FAT HEAD—Stop whatever it is your trying to do regarding my dad. You have been asked before now I have to Tell you to please knock it off.
>
> We DO NOT want any contact with him. If you keep this up your going to **** UP our relationship. I will not forgive you and I mean it. Your messing with our lives. I want you to Stop this bull s***, now!! My family life does not concern you what so ever. Why, the **** do you keep persisting?
>
> When I've already spoken to you about this?? What are trying to do? Don't you have your own bull s*** to worry about?? I'm so pissed off that you keep going on about this. In case, I wasn't clear before, let it sink in now. Mind your own ****** business and DO NOT try to find my dad. If I should discover that you have ignored this message and keep digging around I will turn on you.
>
> Do you understand?? Stay out of my business and worry about your own b*****. I'm so sick of your nosy ass. You'd better stop or we're over.

I'm not going to go thru my life with someone who f****n opens a can of worms that no one wants just because you want to. I'm so pissed right now. This is ****** B*******!

Fifteen minutes later, Joseph answers Summer's rant:

I must say...this is one of the nastiest e-mails I every gotten....So Foul, I can't believe it came from you...

Once again blown completely out of proportion and I thoroughly misunderstood your mom's and your feelings toward your Dad...

So, definitely hear you "loud & clear"....will never be brought up again.

Wow...I'm deleting your e-mail. Its so harsh & sick!

L8!

This was not the only instance of Summer treating her soon-to-be husband with such disdain and contempt.

Here is Joseph's response to a 2005 conversation that he had with Summer that obviously hurt him:

I am sad...

The things you said yesterday hurt me and you probably don't know why...I called 4 times yesterday and you never even tried to call me... but you would call McGyver...Your phone being dead is no excuse, you have plenty of other phones you could use...if you valued me enough.

I guess you think so little of me...very sad & hurt...I am under a tremendous amount of pressure and now this... I did electrical all day yesterday...my hands are cut, my back hurts just to make some $$$ other than bartending 2 very long shifts....

I don't get it...

Sincerely,

Joseph McStay

Would you stay married to someone who treated you like this? Joseph was obviously a much stronger man than I am.

It is no surprise then that Joseph and Summer were in marriage counseling about the time of their disappearance. Fairly normal for any marriage, and as one can see, this marriage was doomed from the start.

A Woman Adrift: Summer McStay

(aka Summer Lisa Aranda-Martelli, Summer Lisa Aranda Martelli, Summer Aranda, Summer L. Martell, Martelli Lisa Aranda, Lisa Y Aranda, Martelli S. Aranda, Lisa V. Aranda, Lisa V. Aranda Jr., Lisa V. Aranda-Martelli, Lisa V. Arandamartelli, L. S. Arandamartelli, Summer L. Aranda Martelli, Martelli L. Aranda)

I believe that if we can expose the core of this mystery, Summer will be right in the middle of it.

Summer was a third-generation American citizen and was raised in the San Gabriel Valley of Southern California. Her Colombian ancestry is through her maternal great-grandmother, even though she has never been to Colombia. Early news reports, most originating from Mike or his mother, seemed to imply that because Summer was a Colombian woman, drugs must have been involved in the family's disappearance.

Summer's sister Tracy was always fascinated with her sister. "While my sister may have been vain, not wanting to grow older, her motherly instincts were a great example for me. She wouldn't let the kids ever ride in a car without a car seat and was like a big momma bear," she told me. "She was very protective of Gianni and little Joseph and was a very serious mother."

Summer was cited for leaving a child unattended in her car in 2006; however, it appears that this was a minor infraction where she left the vehicle for only a couple of minutes, with Gianni always in full view, and a police officer just happened to be on the scene. More bad luck than bad parenting?

She didn't have many, if any, close friends. She had her own agenda, which most times revolved around her desires and hers alone.

Summer was a lost soul.

While Joseph was the non-confrontational type, Summer was the exact opposite. It was common for her to disown her siblings or mother one minute, and then tell them how much she loved them the next.

This must have been difficult for Joseph, who was on the receiving end of her rage more than once. There is little doubt that Joseph loved Summer very deeply and was devoted to her. The question is, was Summer devoted to Joseph? Was Summer capable of being devoted to anyone? Or, to put it more bluntly, was Summer able to truly love?

In the last chapter, we learned that Summer did not have a healthy, loving relationship with Joseph. It appears that Summer's relationships with her siblings were just as toxic.

These two e-mails to a family member, I believe, reveal a woman in torment, blinded by her own pursuits and desires. Never satisfied or content, she always wanted something more.

The first e-mail was sent following her wedding. She had first invited her family, then suddenly uninvited them:

> Yes, we did it. It was lovely but we really missed you.
>
> Who do you think walked me down the aisle? Everyone has a choice to make, right?
>
> Since, I know you'll end up hearing about this soon enough I think I should tell you just like I told Tracy yesterday—I do not want any further contact with my so called family.
>
> Mother says "I got what I deserve for asking you and her about G's hair," causing you and her to leave and not come back. Tracy says I'm so messed up I should "run to the dr. office and get some meds."
>
> Which brings me to you. Tracy says you agree with her as well. If that's true don't bother to explain just stay away from me.
>
> There is only so much I can take. I'm tired of this constant fighting within our family. It's always my fault so its best if I stay away. I don't want my kids to experience this kind of love. I love my family but its clear we do not get along. You are free to leave with "them" as well, s*** it already feels like your gone.

> So, now you know. I wish you Peace, Love, Happiness always. God Bless

The second message is again written to this family member responding to his answer to her first message:

> Well Brother, we could round and round forever. The bottom line is I don't fit in with you guys and nothing I do will ever change it. Most of the stuff we are talking about is so petty but for our family it's the end of the world.
>
> Someone has to let it go and in this case it's me. In the past I never said to stay away, I just stayed away.
>
> This time I'm saying just stay away. I'm sooooo tired of the same old stuff. I say something everyone gets mad. I can't change the dynamics of our family. I can only work on mine. I don't want my kids to see this kind of family life. I know for you its different, you always get the sweet side of "lollipop," I only get the "fuzzy end."
>
> You have Tracy acting and believing she's your mom and you have mom actually wanting to be your mom. You know nothing about my perspective. So I don't blame you for you views but because we come from such vastly different worlds it doesn't make it any better.
>
> I wish you love and happiness always. I hope in time we can have a relationship that satisfies

both of us. Take care & God Bless. Love in your
heart and Peace in your mind.

Summer's caustic attitude also didn't set well with
Joseph's brother or mother. While his father, Patrick,
says he loved and adored Summer, Joseph's brother
Mike and his mother, Susan, didn't like her. In fact,
it was Mike, in an e-mail to Joseph just after he
went missing, who suggested that Summer might be
drugging Joseph. Here is an excerpt from that e-mail
dated April 4, 2010:

> I met Summer's mom, sister, brother, and
> nephew...
>
> They are worried like crazy. They wanted to
> come to the wedding and Summer turned them
> away.
>
> She's not telling you the truth. She's 43, born
> Virginia Lisa Aranda, not 32 like she tells
> everyone.
>
> This woman has lied to you and may be
> drugging you.
>
> That's why your health is diminishing. She needs
> medication. Some believe that she is bi-polar or
> maybe border line personality disorder.

Did Summer Steal Bear?

According to two people very familiar with
Summer, Bear was not the "Guardian Angel" she

liked to claim. According to these individuals who worked with Summer, Bear was Vick's dog and when Summer moved out she took Bear with her, maybe to spite Vick.

"Summer liked to play the victim," one former co-employee told me. "She would claim that Vick was abusing her but I knew he wasn't. One day she claimed that he locked her out of their Big Bear house in the freezing weather, but I knew this was not true. She was not a nice person and I know for a fact that she took Bear when she left just to hurt him all the more."

Whether or not this is true, we do know that Summer's moral clock was off as she was seeing Joseph for many months while still living with Vick.

Was Summer Involved in Porn?

In May 2010, Summer received a few interesting e-mails from a representative of an amateur pornography site. Here is one of the messages:

To:summergrl@hotmail.com

From: avery steed (averysteed2535@live.com)

Sent: Thu 5/06/10 12:10 AM

To: summergrl@hotmail.com

hi!, long has passed since your last e-mail. i have been working out of the US, and lost some of my addresses from my old computer; i have still, to sort out some of them, but your e-mail caught my attention, and I wanted to know what you've been doing.

As I told you, I have been out for about a month, and just as i got back, my nutty sister laverna (who needs more sex than her husband is able to handle-, told me she found this place, where she assures, she gets almost more that SHE can handle 😊

I am not yet sure if i d given you my page address, which is hrnywyfe.com, where you can go to join. I've met some guys already, last weekend was wild, 😊

To be true, I don't recall where you are, but i hope we can meet soon.

I have a couple of pics—of you I think—, and I like them 😊 Just sign in, and let me know your username.

Hope to see you there.

arianna

It is possible that this could have been a spam message. The garbled English in saying "long time" instead of "a long time" could be a common mistake of Asian and Eastern Europeans who speak English as a second language.

Yet "Arianna" says she had previously communicated with Summer. She also claims that she had "pics" of Summer. What were these pics? Were they of a sexual nature?

These could be spammers tricks to try to spook the reader into responding to a website, but it is equally possible that they could be a response to a previous email written by Summer.

This site, hrnywyfe.com, is an amateur pornographic site where "less than sexually satisfied wives" go to post videos of themselves.

While we could find no account for Summer under any of her names, there was one account listed as SummerGirl that was opened in August of 2009. Thankfully, no pictures or videos had been posted.

A Brother Awry: Mike McStay

Joseph and his brother, Mike "Mikey" McStay, were both very young when their parents divorced. While both went to live with their mother, Susan, it appears that Joseph always tried to maintain a relationship with his dad. As is the case with many divorces, there was friction between his mother and father throughout most of his childhood. When he was 16 years old, according to his father, Patrick, he moved in with his dad who lived near Houston. He chose to live there throughout most of his junior year of high school, where he was number 22 on the school's surf team. He loved to surf.

According to Patrick, he and Joseph had a solid relationship right up to the disappearance. They had been in business together and spoke on the phone almost weekly.

Mike, however, did not remain close to his father, and has in fact gone to great lengths to discredit and belittle him, especially when it comes to his choices surrounding the disappearance.

While Mike was careful with his words when I asked him about his relationship with his father, he made clear his dislike for Patrick. "My father has had many opportunities to be a grandfather to my children and has refused each time," he said.

In addition to the grandparent statement, Mike appears to have a legitimate complaint against his father for the way his dad has handled himself throughout this entire mystery: Choosing to stay in Houston rather than relocate to Southern California to take a hands on approach to the search.

In Patrick's defense, it is possible that he would have been arrested had he traveled to California for the same felony crimes that landed him in jail in Louisiana in 2012.

Throughout this mystery, Mike has claimed that he was close to his brother and that they had maintained a deep sibling relationship. A claim that was disputed by some of Joseph's friends, who believe that Mike has always, to some extent, been jealous of Joseph.

It appears that Mike had a difficult time making it on his own financially. At times, unable to support his family of five, he turned to his half brother for financial assistance. According to Summer's family, Mike was at their house often asking for money and Summer was beginning to let her displeasure be known. She had claimed to her sister that Joseph had loaned Mike over $10,000. Summer had had more than one major confrontation with Mike about his "habitual borrowing with no intent of ever paying it back," according to her family.

This alleged behavior appears to have accelerated shortly after the disappearance.

Joseph had only been gone a month when Mike transferred $5,000 out of Joseph's bank account and into his own account, without permission, of course.

According to Dan Kavanaugh, Joseph's former webmaster and pseudo business associate, soon after the disappearance, Mike also began to intercept Joseph's receivables from his profitable fountain business.

"Mike and his dad are nothing but money grabbers," said Kavanaugh. "Joey hadn't been gone a week when Mike wanted all the contact information for Joey's receivables. He called them and told them to send the check to him. I know he got one check for $15,000."

Here is just one of the intercepts of Joseph's funds by Mike. Note that the email address md@precisionfiresystems.com is Mike McStay's.

eCheck payment in progress

3/25/10

To Earth Inspired Products

From: service@paypal.com (service@paypal.com)

Sent: Thu 3/25/10 3:51 PM

To: Earth Inspired Products (josephmcstay69@hotmail.com)

PayPal

Hello Earth Inspired Products,

Your eCheck payment of $5,000.00 USD to EarthInspiredProducts.com (md@ precisionfiresystems.com) is in progress. eChecks usually take 3-5 business days to process (estimated: 3/30/2010-4/1/2010). We advise merchants not to ship items until they receive payment.

Payment details

Amount: $5,000.00 USD

Transaction Date: Mar 25, 2010

Transaction ID: 7AG806806B413274P

Subject: Paul Mitchell Order (CaseStack Payment)

There is also the question of where the $81,000 for the Saudi fountain went. Joseph's policy was a fifty percent deposit with the balance due on completion. The Saudi fountain was ordered on January 16, 2010 and would have taken about five weeks for the order to be completed, meaning that $40,500 would have come into EIP the end of February. The remaining $40,500 would then be paid upon installation, which was completed by Joseph's business associate in May. Who got the money? Did Mike deposit it into one of Joseph's business accounts or did he keep it himself?

Throughout the book, we see example after example of a brother who claims to love and miss his sibling, only to behave in a way that contradicts his words.

On March 16, 2010, Mike registered EarthInspiredProducts.com. Joseph's company was Earth Inspired Products. This appears that Mike was attempting to take over his brother's company. We will learn that he already had all of Joseph's passwords to his PayPal and business bank accounts by this time, so what was his motivation for registering this name?

The first week of April, 2010, Mike sent a long, rambling email to Joseph. Here are a few lines from his quickly composed message:

"I've been by your side since the beginning... from Santo, to Houston, to Northern Calif."

"Through thick and thin. I've whipped some ass for you.... you're a good brother."

"I hope your health is ok.. I know that your balance has been off...."

"We're keeping your business going and your house."

But was Mike really keeping the business and Joseph's house going as he claimed?

Why did it take Mike eleven days to call law enforcement?

Once the missing persons report had been filed, Mike joined many of the online sleuth websites. On one those sites, InSessions.com, Mike was given contacts he could call to help find his brother. He did not contact them.

When many members started questioning him about the inconsistency of his statements, he didn't answer and just stopped posting.

"He'd go on TV and say one thing, then he'd go on a different program and say something else and then he would be interviewed by a newspaper and contradict his two earlier statements and we began to question his honesty," said one longtime sleuth member.

If my brother went missing, I would be begging for help from experts and organizing flyer distribution on February 15. Actually, that is not correct, because I would have known my brother disappeared long before Mike claims he knew. Eleven days is hard to believe.

Some have claimed that Mike knows exactly what happened that Thursday night and this and other emails he sent to Joseph after the disappearance were staged. Law enforcement has never commented on whether or not they asked Mike for his whereabouts on February 4, or if they have ever looked at his bank accounts.

We do know however, that Mike had Joseph's computer for some time. How long, we don't know. Mike claims that he only had the computer for a day or two before law enforcement realized he had taken it and threatened to arrest him unless he brought it back.

If Mike actually had taken the computer on Saturday, February 6, and not the week of the 15th as he has claimed, he would have had plenty of time to get into Joseph's email accounts and financial institutions and alter them. Joseph made it a habit of emailing to himself all of his passwords. So Mike had access to all of Joseph's financial accounts from PayPal, to his business accounts at Wells Fargo and Union Bank. Did Mike delete certain emails from Joseph's account that might have shed light on this mystery? We will never know because he had the computer before law enforcement did.

If Mike does know, he has never let on in any email to his brother or Summer, realizing now that they were being monitored by law enforcement.

I believe that law enforcement knew four months into the disappearance that something wasn't right. It was about that time that detectives stopped communicating with Mike as they had early on. Had Mike's behavior caused suspicion with law enforcement?

Did Detective Dugal's curious statements to America's Most Wanted in June of 2010 reveal just that?

When asked by the host for his theory on the mystery he said, "I hope it's voluntary missing but I have to believe it's worse than that." Had law enforcement already determined that they most likely had a murder investigation on their hands?

This could explain one reason why detectives have been almost silent on this case in the last two years. Are they waiting for someone to slip up or looking for a body?

Mike McStay is one of the main players in this case. In a later chapter, we will learn that just a few months after the disappearance, Mike went to Joseph's house, loaded up all of Joseph and Summer's possessions of value and sold everything on Ebay and Craig's List. He has made conflicting statements to the media, confused facts, and displayed a type of behavior that leads one to question his actions after his brother went missing.

The Six Days Before

There is a plethora of news articles available on the Internet detailing the mystery of the missing McStay family, and all of them begin with February 4, 2010, the last day anyone has ever heard from the family—or at least this is what we are led to believe.

While only Joseph and Summer know for sure what happened after this day, we have uncovered a great deal of information about what went on in their family life the six days before their disappearance.

A close examination of this period has helped to put the McStays' week in context and has also brought to light new information confirming my belief that some individuals may not have told the complete truth from the beginning. They know, but are still withholding information about this mystery even today.

We begin by returning to Friday night, January 29. According to Mike McStay, Joseph was seen engaging in a curious conversation with two men right after his soccer game in Aliso Viejo in southern Orange County. According to Mike, the conversation was heated and had to do with a purchase that Summer had made from craigslist. Her e-mails show that she had bought the popular Rosetta Stone software, a language-learning aid, and needed to set up delivery.

However, I spoke with one of Joseph's best soccer friends, and he denies this conversation ever took place, at least a heated one.

"I was with Joseph three nights a week, Monday, Wednesday, and Friday nights. After soccer we would go eat or have a drink. I never saw Joey talking to these two men ever in the month of January 2010. The only way he could have had that conversation was if these guys were waiting for him at his car, he gave them a hundred bucks, and was on his way in ten seconds. There was no conversation that got heated, at least not in January."

We know the purchase was made because the box was found in the McStays' home. This was Summer's second purchase of Spanish language software. She had already used Joseph's eBay account to buy a different brand of children's Spanish-learning software in July 2009.

The next night, Saturday, January 30, reveals more clues to this mystery when at about 8:00 p.m., Summer calls a close family friend to vent about that evening's dinner guest.

McGyver McGargar had been a friend of both Joseph and Summer for many years. He was the one who introduced them, was part of their wedding, and was the family confidant. McGyver was also the only person to have spent three of the four days with the McStays before they went missing.

McGyver and I devoted many hours rebuilding those three days spent at the McStays' home in Fallbrook. Much of the insight that we now have about how the McStays spent their final days comes directly from this family friend. Were Summer and Joseph getting along? Were they planning a trip? Were they having financial troubles? What was really going on with their external family members? What was the condition of their home during this final week versus when the police would enter the home two weeks later? Had the home been staged by someone else during those two weeks?

When Summer called McGyver on that Saturday night, it was to complain about one of Joseph's business associates who had been their dinner guest that evening. Summer was furious with some of this man's opinions about how she was raising their children and needed to talk to someone. Apparently, this man told Summer that she needed to have both of the kids vaccinated, and this sent Summer over the edge. "You will not tell me how to raise my kids," she told this man with a forceful voice.

"Summer certainly had her opinions," McGyver told me. "And trying to tell her how to raise her kids was not the smart thing to do!"

During the conversation, Summer told McGyver that she was painting the interior of their home and that her painter had not returned from a business trip. She said she wanted to finish the painting before Joseph Junior's birthday party the next Saturday, February 6. McGyver offered to help paint that next day, and she was thankful for his help.

"So on Sunday, I head down to their house and paint all day. I painted the living room and most of the kitchen while Summer and Joseph were playing with the kids. It was kind of frustrating that Summer didn't even help me," said McGyver.

"Later, we just all sat down and chilled. Joseph told me about his funky illness, how he wasn't feeling well and didn't know what to do about it. His dizzy spells were getting worse, and the doctor couldn't find the reason. Summer couldn't stop talking about a new pizza place they'd found off Highway 395 in the Comfort Inn, Fallbrook," recalled McGyver.

McGyver remembered that they spent time on the floor playing with Bear. "Bear was so big but had such a great heart and was great with the kids," said McGyver. "Summer really loved Bear. She said that he was her guardian angel and that she wouldn't go anywhere without him."

After a day of painting on Sunday, the painting was still unfinished. "I told Summer I'd come back down that next day on Monday," said McGyver. However, when he learned that he had an unexpected conflict on Monday and wouldn't be available again until Tuesday, he texted Summer to reschedule and was stunned at her reaction.

"When I texted Summer to tell her I couldn't be there Monday but would come back on Tuesday instead, she blew up. She accused me of not being her friend and used words I can't repeat. I was really shocked and didn't know what was going on with her. Summer was always a bit of a Mrs. Jekyll and Mrs. Hyde to me, but this was bizarre."

McGyver returned to finish the painting on Tuesday, as promised, and worked half the day. This was now just two days before they would vanish. Did McGyver sense anything different about Summer or Joseph on that Tuesday?

"She didn't talk to me all day," said McGyver. "I think she was embarrassed over the way she treated me in her angry text conversations on Sunday night, but other than that, it was just life as usual for the McStays."

By Tuesday at noon, it was obvious the painting would not be finished, and even though McGyver was getting frustrated over how long it was taking, he agreed to return one more time that next day, Wednesday. "I could only work half the day on Wednesday but figured that would finish the painting. It was really getting old," said McGyver.

Also on Tuesday, Summer bought a children's playhouse from a seller on craigslist for $200, though we don't know the specifics of whether it was to be delivered or picked up by Summer or Joseph.

On Wednesday morning when McGyver arrived, Joseph was at the house. He had been busy working on a long-term contract that would supposedly net him millions. "He told me that a big corporation was buying over five hundred car washes in the country, and they wanted him to design and install fountains in each one," said McGyver. "He said it was a huge deal."

According to Joseph's father, had Joseph built those five hundred fountains, he would have netted more than three million dollars over the next seven years.

As McGyver was painting the living room, he suddenly heard Joseph outside chastising his kids for something. He headed outside to see what all the fuss was about. Gianni and Joseph Junior had apparently taken the paintbrushes from inside and had painted Joseph's green Dodge pickup truck with nice beige interior latex. "It was kind of funny, really," said McGyver. "But Joseph handled it well. He was miffed but started cleaning his truck before the paint dried. He was a great dad."

At about noon on Wednesday, McGyver cleaned his painting equipment and sat down on the family futon, frustrated that the painting was still not complete. "I'll come back again tomorrow," said McGyver, "and that should do it." He spent the next hour or so on the futon catching up with his buddy Joseph. Joseph told him how the house remodel was basically Summer's project and how excited she was the way it was all coming together. He told McGyver that he would start on the car wash contract that next week after Little Joseph's birthday party on Saturday.

"When I left their house on Wednesday afternoon, Joseph was stoked, Summer was happy, and the kids were having a blast being kids," observed McGyver.

Yet later that evening, Summer texted McGyver and told him not to come back that next day, Thursday. "Take a break and come back Saturday, not tomorrow. We'll finish it then. You are such a best friend, McGyver, thanks," read her text message that he had saved in his iPhone.

A multimillion dollar contract, a house on the path to being remodeled, a happy family of four, and yet in just thirty-three hours, they would vanish.

"I texted Summer on Friday and asked her what time for Saturday," said McGyver. "There was no return text, so I called her cell, and it went directly into her voice mail. I still hadn't heard from her by Friday night, so I called Joseph, and his phone went into voice mail as well. They never returned my calls, and I have never heard from them again."

The questions are now beginning to mount: Why did Summer move the painting to Saturday, the day of the "alleged" birthday party, when the house was sure to be full of chaos, or was the party somewhere else? What was the "funky illness" that Joseph had talked about with McGyver? Why did Summer leave her guardian angel, Bear, behind?

Thursday, February 4, 2010

Do you know what you were doing on February 4, 2010? If you were forced, could you reconstruct that day in your life hour by hour, minute by minute? It would probably be a challenge for you as it would be for me.

I believe that this day, the last day that the McStays have been seen or heard from, holds many keys to what happened to this family. Did they voluntarily vanish as the California Department of Justice believes, or was their disappearance more sinister? Are they living on a Caribbean beach, travelling up and down the East Coast surfing, or are they buried in shallow graves?

A thorough examination of Joseph and Summer's e-mails, credit card receipts, financial and bank records, phone messages, conversations with friends, and computer records has revealed that Thursday, February 4, 2010, appears, on its surface, to be just another busy day in the lives of the McStays.

Summer's Day

Summer's sister told me that she believed Summer rose early that morning to begin working on their son's birthday party that was said to be held at the local Chuck E. Cheese's pizza emporium. Joseph Junior had turned three years old on January 31, and they were having the delayed party on Saturday, February 6.

At 9:00 a.m., Summer called her sister and made plans to drive the sixty miles north to San Bernardino to see her and her newborn son sometime that next week.

McGyver believes that because he wasn't able to finish the interior painting the day before, Summer pulled off the party planning at about 10:00 a.m. to wrap up the painting in time for the party. They didn't have any Fallbrook friends yet, but Summer told McGyver that many of their longtime friends from San Clemente were coming to the party and that Summer wanted to showcase their new home following the party.

However, according to one of her friends (who wishes to remain unnamed), there was no party. "I never heard about any party and wasn't invited to see their house either. If there was a party, I would have been invited. Plus, Summer hated the house, so I'm not sure why anyone would think she would want to showcase it anyway."

Not one of these friends who were supposed to show up for the party ever reported going to Chuck E. Cheese's on Saturday and that Summer was not there, nor have they ever reported that they went to the house on Saturday and no one was home. So it appears that the party had been cancelled, or it was never planned at all.

At 2:11 p.m., Summer made her last cell phone call on one of her two mobile phones to a homeopathic medicine company, and an employee remembered it well. It came minutes after an Internet search on the home computer for the word *anger* on the company website. According to Detective Dugal, the employee said that Summer wanted to purchase a medication that did not exist called Anger.

"She was adamant about purchasing that medication, and I said, 'Ma'am, it doesn't exist.'"

Apparently, Summer had not remembered the exact name of the medication, referring to it only as anger, and so the employee could not help her. The medication she was looking at online is actually called Anger-Soothe.

According to the website, the medication is a "safe, non-addictive, FDA-registered natural remedy containing 100% homeopathic ingredients selected to relieve feelings of anger and irritability, including fits of rage and temper outbursts."

The site claims that Anger-Soothe can be used to "safely support the nervous system at a cellular level, and relieve feelings of frustration and discontent without harmful side effects. This remedy contains a selection of homeopathic ingredients known for their ability to address emotions causing anger, irritability and temper outbursts."

Was Summer angry? I believe she was, as we will learn.

In mid-afternoon, Summer apparently went shopping. Her credit card was used at the Ross Department Store in Vista, a town just west of

Fallbrook, at 2:36 p.m. It is interesting to note that evidence of this transaction didn't surface until almost a year after this day. Any surveillance video had long been erased. Law enforcement has never commented on why it took them a year to find this transaction.

We only know that someone used Summer's credit card to charge $66 at the store and that they purchased beach bags, infant pajamas, and a jacket. Family members of both Summer and Joseph have viewed the digital signature, and no one believes the signature belongs to either Summer or Joseph. At any rate, because the signature was made on an electronic touch pad, it would not be a valid representation for comparison.

The only transaction on her credit card that day was the Ross purchase. It appears that she left Ross in Vista (if this was indeed Summer who made the purchase) and headed home.

However, this cannot be correct.

According to the detective, Summer's last cell call was at 2:11 p.m. just after she, or someone, had been on the home computer looking at the anger medication website. Her credit card was run, according to Ross, at 2:36 p.m., just twenty-five minutes after her cell phone call. This is not possible.

I drove from the McStays' house to the Ross in Vista on a Thursday at the same time of day. It took me twenty-nine minutes the first time and thirty-four minutes the next, and I was driving my Maserati. This was backing out of their driveway, parking at the Ross in Vista, and entering the front door. That allows no time to shop, head to the checkout, and run the credit card.

Someone's facts are wrong. Either the cell phone company had their time wrong, or Ross had their time wrong. The only other possibility is that the second Summer had finished reading about the anger medication on the computer, she rushed to the truck and headed to Ross, calling the employee while she was driving and forgetting the exact name of the medication, which would explain the employee's comments. But that doesn't work either as she would have to make the trip in less than twenty minutes, which is not possible, even with no traffic.

Something happened between 3:52 p.m., when Summer was on the computer, and 4:25 p.m. when she called Joseph from their landline. While law enforcement has never revealed the computer activity during that timeframe, we do know that Joseph is now back in the Fallbrook area because his call pinged off a Fallbrook cell tower. Law enforcement had also stated that Joseph bought gas in the area during that timeframe.

What was it that possibly set everything in motion? Was it an e-mail or a text? Who was it from? Had she opened the mail she had retrieved that morning?

Whatever it was, she felt compelled enough to immediately call Joseph. We don't know how long the call lasted.

But Summer had another cell phone with a second number. She used it to call a business associate on that Thursday at 11:00 a.m. According to the associate, Summer had just acquired the new phone in the past couple of days. The number, 760-412-7436, is no longer working. We were never able to secure the phone logs for that number.

Joseph's Day

We don't know what Joseph did with his morning. It has been reported that he worked on the countertops in the bathroom or kitchen and installed the new appliances, but we know from an earlier video in December 2009 that these counters and appliances were already installed.

We do know that around noon, Joseph headed to the Rancho Cucamonga area for a lunch appointment with his business associate. He told Summer that he'd be back by dark, around 5:30 p.m.

After lunch at about 2:00 p.m., Joseph headed back south to Fallbrook, about a two-hour drive with traffic. Along the way he stopped at the bank and deposited a $16,000 check that he had picked up for a job he had completed.

Between 4:00 p.m. and 5:00 p.m., Joseph pulled off the Interstate 15 freeway because he was feeling ill. We know this because he called his mother to tell her he was enduring another mysterious dizzy spell, though we don't know where he was on the interstate in relation to his home.

Here is an e-mail from Joseph to a friend in November 2009 about his mystery illness:

> From: J McStay (josephmcstay69@hotmail.com)
>
> Sent: Wed 11/11/09 2:48 PM

To: agxxxxx@xxxxx.com

Head in a vice up & down like a yo yo...sucks....
but, signing docs at 5:30 today...

Yes...yahoo is eipfountains@yahoo.com

thats it...just want to get back to health...&
play soccer 3 days a week.... They just came out
all over news.... It's confirmed cell phones are
causing cancer.... we knew this, now confirmed....
I wonder if this has to do with my head? since
i always have it on my ear instead of speaker or
manual headset? I'm so stupid... i drive with it in
between my shoulder & head... doip!

Sincerely,

Joseph McStay

Joseph's father, Patrick, claims that law enforcement
investigators told him Joseph bought gas near his home
at about 4:30 p.m. and that he paid for a prescription
for the kids, Amoxicillin, at a local pharmacy at about
the same time.

Joseph and Summer texted each other at 5:00 p.m.
and 5:47 p.m. respectively, so we can assume Joseph was
not at the house yet.

We don't know what was in the texts. The San
Diego sheriff's department claims that it was not able
to subpoena the transcripts of these texts, so no one
knows what was written in these messages, and the
texts have probably long been deleted from the servers.

Was Summer asking when Joseph would be home? We don't know for certain that Joseph ever arrived home that night. No neighbor or other witness can place Joseph at his house that evening.

We can speculate that Summer was probably getting dinner ready and that Joseph returned home by about 6:15 p.m. Maybe they discuss the matter of concern to Summer. It goes longer than anticipated. Summer fixes the boys popcorn to hold them over until dinner. They discuss up until about 7:45 p.m.

One theory holds that they departed the home and headed west on Highway 76 toward Oceanside. As they passed the San Luis Rey riverbed area, they ditched their cell phones determining at this point, there was no return. There is no evidence that they ever ditched their cell phones in the riverbed, only that Joseph's cell pinged off a tower near that area.

We do know that at 7:47 p.m., a neighbor's surveillance video captured the McStays' Isuzu Trooper pulling out from the driveway, but the angle of the camera only shows the vehicle's tires and doors. We cannot see the windows or who is in the vehicle. We confirmed that Joseph had driven the Trooper to his lunch meeting with his business associate, so it is assumed he was at home and driving.

Did the neighbor's cameras record the Trooper returning that evening? According to Mike, a "glitch in the neighbor's computer systems left no surveillance footage from midnight February 4 through late on Monday night, February 15." But this is not an accurate statement. I spoke to the neighbor, and she confirmed to me that her computer systems were *not* down from midnight of February 4 through late Monday night, February 15, as Mike has previously stated. Why would Mike not tell the truth about the video cameras?

At 8:28 p.m., Joseph's cell phone records a one-minute call. It has been reported by law enforcement that this call was to a business associate in Rancho Cucamonga to discuss an upcoming job. We cannot even be certain that Joseph talked to anyone. This call did ping off a Fallbrook cell tower again but was likely not made from their home, though this cannot be proven either.

This was the last call ever made from Joseph's cell phone.

And that was the last anyone has ever heard from the McStay family.

Or was it?

What about Summer's cell phone? Did it ping again later that evening or the next day as some have claimed? Was it not turned off and received other text messages, for example the ones sent from her friend McGyver? To this day, law enforcement has never offered an answer to this question.

The Week After

As I sat on the floor of my studio with over a hundred documents strategically placed around me trying to build a timeline, one truth quickly became evident. If the McStays really wanted to just disappear, they could have pulled it off.

While the famous border-crossing video is not likely the McStay family as many have claimed, they could have moved to Mexico and be living near a beach where Joseph spends his days catching the perfect wave.

It is not illegal in the United States for a family to just up and move. There is no law that demands they tell family members or ask permission. To me, this case has never been about whether they left voluntarily. It has been about *why* they would leave voluntarily.

We have been told that everything was going well for the McStays, and they had no reason to leave. On the surface, they were a happy and content family with money in the bank, two growing businesses, and good friendships. We know they were in the middle of remodeling their dream house. However, a deeper look inside this family reveals a bitter discontent, businesses in turmoil, and shallow friendships.

So what if the skeptics are correct, and they didn't leave voluntarily after all? What if something more sinister, more evil, engulfed the family? Soon after the disappearance, the police announced that they believed the McStays decided to just move away and not tell anyone. More than once, the sheriff's department has claimed that they have "overwhelming circumstantial evidence" that Joseph and his family had voluntarily gone to Mexico.

A year or so later, the SDSD stated that they still believed they went to Mexico, but something "bad" might have happened to them there.

Many critics have claimed that because law enforcement believed from the beginning that the family left voluntarily, they might not have treated the home, or other evidence, in the way they would had a murder or abduction taken place. The actions that followed two weeks after the McStays disappearance—from Friday, February 5, through Friday, February 19—leans toward apathy by law enforcement and possible criminal interference by family members.

We begin on Friday, February 5, the day after they vanished.

Joseph's father, Patrick, has claimed that he spoke with his son on the phone three or four times a week on different days and at different times. There are no unaltered phone records to confirm this claim, and so we only know what Patrick says. He says that Joseph called him most every Friday night on his way to his soccer league in San Clemente. These conversations could be short or last up to forty-five minutes. On

Friday, February 5, when Joseph didn't call his dad as usual, Patrick called Joseph, and his cell went directly into voice mail. "I didn't leave a message. I never left messages because I knew Joseph would see my name on his caller ID," said Patrick.

On Saturday, there was still no return phone call to Patrick from Joseph. "I was a little concerned at this point because we always spoke on Friday night, but I just assumed he was busy and would get to me when he was free."

When Patrick still had not heard from Joseph by Sunday, he called Joseph's cell again and this time left a message asking for a return call.

There was no word from Joseph on Monday, but Patrick did receive a phone call from the San Diego area on Tuesday that would later become an integral part of this case. The caller's ID was D. Kavanaugh, a name that Patrick didn't recognize, so he didn't answer it. Later on Tuesday afternoon, he received an e-mail from the same person, which he immediately deleted, believing it to be spam.

On Tuesday morning, February 9, Patrick had now been out of contact with Joseph for five days and was worried. "This was not normal for Joseph, so I called Mike and asked him to go to Joseph's house to check on the family," said Patrick.

Mike wasn't surprised that Patrick hadn't heard from Joseph as he claims that it wasn't uncommon for the family to take a long weekend without alerting anyone. But is this true?

Patrick says that Joseph always called him on Friday nights, whether in town or on a family excursion. Plus, hadn't they planned a birthday party for little Joseph on that Saturday?

Mike told Patrick that he was "too busy" and didn't have time to check on his brother, which Patrick found odd. "When he told me he was busy, I basically told him to get his rear end down there now because no one has heard from the family since last Thursday, and I didn't care how busy he was."

Patrick told Mike that the only calls he had received with a San Diego area code were from a D. Kavanaugh and that he didn't know who that was. "You know who that is, Dad. That's Dan the Hacker. He used to work with Joseph," said Mike. Mike said he would call Dan to find out why he was calling Patrick and then get right back to him.

What Patrick could not have been aware of at this point in the mystery was that before Dan Kavanaugh had called him on Monday, he had systematically begun to withdraw thousands of dollars from Joseph's bank account without permission. On Saturday, February 6, three days before he would call Patrick, Kavanaugh would initiate a withdrawal of $2,000 from Joseph's business account by apparently hacking into it to gain Joseph's password. He would withdraw another $2,000 from Joseph's account on Monday, February 15, and then $3,000 just three days later on Thursday, February 18. For some reason, investigators failed to lock down Joseph's bank accounts.

During the same period that Kavanaugh was transferring money out of Joseph's account and into his own, there were attempts made to gain access to Joseph's financial QuickBooks account stored at the Intuit.com online database.

On Monday, February 8, someone tried to download Joseph's entire online business account using the wrong password. On Wednesday, February 10, the day Mike was going to Joseph's house to check on the family, someone again tried to gain access to his account with a fraudulent password. Finally, the very next day, someone contacted Intuit.com, where Joseph stored his QuickBooks database, and asked the company to send a CD of the entire account to an address in San Clemente, California, which was the former home of Joseph and Summer. Intuit refused, but a new copy of QuickBooks was ordered.

Further, on Friday, February 12, Joseph received an e-mail from Wells Fargo alerting him that someone had changed the mailing address for his Wells Fargo business account.

Mike called his father back after he talked to Kavanaugh, who, according to Mike, claimed he was concerned that he hadn't heard from Joseph since February 4. Did Mike know at this point that Dan had been systematically withdrawing thousands of dollars from Joseph's business accounts?

Who was trying to access Joseph's financial records, and why was Mike seemingly not concerned about his brother's whereabouts?

Aside: Patrick has been widely criticized for not jumping on an airplane and heading to Fallbrook to learn firsthand what had happened to his son, relying instead on Mike for information. I think that is not fair to Patrick. At this point in the disappearance, the money transfers and other pertinent information were not known, and it was possible that Joseph and family had indeed just taken a mini vacation.

Mike finally agreed to go to Joseph's house that next day, Wednesday, February 10, and would call his dad later that day. "He told me that he couldn't get into the house because it was locked, that the Trooper was gone but Joseph's green Dodge pickup was in the driveway," said Patrick. "He also told me that both Bear and Digger were in the backyard and that a neighbor must have given them food and water so they were okay."

But in fact, Mike had not gone to the house.

The San Diego sheriff's department official timeline in this case shows that a business associate of Joseph's had called the police on Wednesday to check on the family's welfare. This "business associate" was actually Dan Kavanaugh, not Mike. The report states that there was "no answer at the door" and "no signs of foul play."

How did Kavanaugh miss the notice on the front door from Animal Control? The notice explained that neighbors had contacted them because the dogs had been barking incessantly for days and had apparently been left with no food and water. The Animal Control officer left food and water in the backyard and requested a phone call to their office.

Why would Mike not be truthful with his father? What did Mike know about Joseph's disappearance? This is just one of many inconsistencies in Mike's statements to police as well as the media. Does this mean that Mike was in on a plot to hurt the family or that Mike helped his brother disappear?

Mike did actually go to the house on Saturday, February 13, when it appeared he gained access through an unlocked window.

It is important to note that Mike has told three different stories to the media about how he got into Joseph's house. First, he told the *Los Angeles Times* on February 21 that he "broke in a back window" to enter the house. Then he changed his story to other media outlets when he said he found a "partially open window," then his story changed again when he told me on *The Rick and Becky Radio Show* that he found an "unlocked window" and entered there. "There have been many unfounded rumors that I broke a window to get into Joseph's house, which is not true," Mike told us on our show. "I have never said that."

It was on February 13, not February 10, that Mike told Patrick about the notice on the door from Animal Control, a notice that had been posted on Monday, February 8. Patrick now knew that Mike had not been at the house on Wednesday as he claimed.

Mike told his dad that they weren't going to call the police until Monday, the day after Valentine's Day, because Joseph and Summer were probably "just out on a long weekend."

Yet he was in the house on February 13, nine days after the family had disappeared, and as he would state later, it was obvious to him that his brother had left in a hurry. Not an "extended weekend" as he had first claimed.

When Mike saw the unsettled condition of the house, why would he not call the sheriff's department immediately? He wouldn't, of course, if he was the one doing the ransacking. What was Mike looking for on that Saturday afternoon? What was he looking for inside Joseph and Summer's home?

As Patrick began to do the math, Mike's extended weekend scenario didn't make sense to him. This was no long weekend. "It had been nine days since they were last heard from," said Patrick. "What about little Joseph's birthday party on Saturday, February 6? Why would they leave before his party? Something was just not adding up," thought Patrick at that time. "I wasn't sure what it was, only that Mike was not telling me everything."

On Monday, February 15, Mike would return to Joseph's house and then call the police. The official report reveals that deputies did a quick sweep of the house, which supposes that Mike had arrived before law enforcement, entered again through the back window, and let in the deputies.

The deputies then called homicide detectives because of the length of time that Joseph and his family had been unaccounted for as well as the "condition of the house."

Whatever the sheriff's department found in the house caused them to issue a bulletin to the press that the family had vanished.

Had Joseph and Summer's house been staged to make it look like a voluntary disappearance? Is this the reason Mike didn't call the police when his dad first asked him to on Wednesday, February 10? Did he call Kavanaugh and have him go instead? And if so, why? Why did it take him an additional five days to report his brother and his family as missing?

Eleven Days and No Answer

By Monday, February 15, Joseph and his family had been missing for eleven days with no answers but only more questions, many of them relating directly to Joseph's brother, Mike.

Why did Mike ignore his father's concerns when he couldn't contact Joseph for days? Why did Mike tell his dad he went to Joseph's house on February 10 when it appears he did not? Why did it take Mike an extra five days to report Joseph missing? Why did Mike tell differing stories about how he entered Joseph's house? Was he just not keen on the details, or was there some other reason? How long was Mike in the house on Saturday, February 13, and what was he looking for?

While these questions are curious and have yet to be answered by Mike himself, it is his behavior in these next four days, February 15–19, that should bring pause.

We know that Mike called the San Diego sheriff's department to report Joseph and his family missing on Monday afternoon, February 15, a full eleven days after they had disappeared. We know that Mike had entered

Joseph's house again to let in the two deputies, who briefly walked throughout the house.

These deputies then called in homicide detectives based on the circumstances of the case: A family had been gone for eleven days with no word to family or friends. Their two four-legged family members, Bear and Digger, had been left in the backyard. Remember, Bear was Summer's "guardian angel," and she never left him behind. Then there was the odd condition of the house: A popcorn bag had been left in the kitchen along with two child-sized bowls of popcorn in the living room. A carton of eggs were still on the kitchen counter. It appeared that the family left in a hurry.

Two hours after the deputies entered the house, bulletins with pictures of the family and their Isuzu Trooper were sent to law enforcement and news agencies in the United States and Mexico. The sheriff's department was now concerned that a crime may have been committed after all.

Almost immediately after the bulletins were sent, Joseph's Trooper was found. It had been towed from a parking lot in a strip mall on the border at San Ysidro, California, at 11:00 p.m. on Monday, February 8. The owners of the strip mall claimed that the Trooper had been parked there between 5:30 p.m. and 7:00 p.m. on Monday night, four days after the McStays vanished, and that they had it towed at 11:00 p.m. We would find out months later that this information was not correct.

In order for the sheriff's department to confiscate the Trooper or any contents from the home, such as their computers or bank records, they needed a warrant.

The original detective on this case, Lt. Dennis Brugos (who has since retired from the department), told Mike that it would take about four days to get the warrant, and they would be back on Friday, February 19.

So on the night of February 15, 2010, the house and the Trooper became official "crime scenes." For the next four days, the house and vehicle were off-limits to everyone. Or were they?

When Joseph's dad, Patrick, learned from deputies that a possible crime had been committed, he called Texas EquuSearch Mounted Search and Recovery Team. This search organization (www.texasequusarch. org) was founded by Tim Miller in 2000 after his daughter, Laura Miller, was abducted and murdered in 1984. It is highly respected and has been involved in over 1,100 searches with their efforts resulting in returning over 300 missing persons to their families and loved ones.

Patrick felt that it was very important to search the area around Joseph and Summer's house as it backs up to a large open area and a dry riverbed that had been inhabited by many illegal immigrants. Fallbrook, as is the case with much of California, has a large population of illegal immigrants. Patrick was concerned that someone had come up out of the riverbed and abducted or harmed the family, and he wanted the area searched. Once Tim Miller learned that the Trooper had been found on the border, he wanted to use a drone aircraft to search the entire sixty-mile area from the border to the house.

The search of the house and area would be scheduled for the coming weekend once the warrants were secured.

In an apparent oversight, the sheriff's department failed to properly secure the house and Dodge pickup as a crime scene. The pickup was left unlocked in the driveway with a video camera in open view on the seat, and the house was not sealed.

What happened next is hard to explain.

It was Wednesday afternoon, February 17, two days after the house was officially made a crime scene, that Joseph's mother, Susan, called family friend McGyver. She asked him to meet her at Joseph's house because she wanted to get some of his things, and she was afraid to be there by herself. (A neighbor confirmed to me that a woman matching the description of Susan was at the house that afternoon.)

"I said that I would meet her there and drove down that evening," recalls McGyver.

It was what he saw when he got there that, to this day, makes no sense to him. "When I got to the house, Susan was busy cleaning the kitchen. She had just cleaned the kitchen countertop and was for some reason almost in a panic as she appeared to be searching the house for something. I asked her what she needed me to do, and she told me to look for all bank statements," said McGyver.

"I found one bank account statement that had a large balance, and so I gave it to her," said McGyver.

McGyver had not been privy to everything that happened that previous Monday. He didn't know the house had been declared a crime scene; he didn't know

Joseph's Trooper had been found on the border. He was just there to help the mother of one of his best friends.

"I did think it was kind of weird that Susan was cleaning up so quickly and kind of panicking. She was really working fast. I asked her if the police had been here yet, and she said that they had been."

McGyver had been the last known person to be at the McStay home on Wednesday, February 3, the day before they disappeared. On that day he had been throughout the house, upstairs and downstairs. Now he instantly noticed that the condition of the house was very different from the last time he had been there.

"What was really strange was that the futon Joseph and I had sat on that Wednesday afternoon was on the floor, out of its frame, and the cover for the futon was missing. That was odd. What happened to the cover?

"I also noticed that someone had pushed the paint roller and tray that I had used earlier under a chair. It had dried paint in it, so I knew that someone had done some painting on Thursday, February 4, because I had cleaned it before I left a day earlier."

McGyver toured the house in search of the bank statements that Susan wanted, as well as the missing futon cover. When he went into Joseph and Summer's master bedroom, he was shocked.

"There were clothes and shoes all over the floor, and the room was a mess," he said. "It looked to me like someone had gone through all their things. That room didn't look like that when I was there on February 3."

I asked McGyver if he ever found the futon cover and if he searched the house thoroughly. "Nope, I never found it, and I looked everywhere," he told me. "That is still very strange to me."

Another oddity is that Mike claims that he took Joseph's computer sometime before Friday, February 19. A source told me that once law enforcement learned of this, they asked Mike if he knew where it was. He admitted to having taken it and was told that unless he returned it immediately, he faced arrest for taking crime scene evidence.

I asked Mike about Joseph's computer when he was interviewed on our show, and he told us that the police had allowed him to take the computer home. "The deputies said I could take it home and check them out because I was his brother."

So more questions: Why was Susan cleaning the kitchen and other areas? Did she not realize that she was contaminating a crime scene? Was she embarrassed that her daughter-in-law was a slob? And what happened to the futon cover?

Many of these questions might have been answered if someone other than Mike had asked the neighbor with the surveillance cameras to review all her video from the morning of February 5 through February 15. What would those tapes have shown? The neighbor told me that she "just didn't want to get involved," and so valuable evidence may have been lost.

Had the sheriff's department subpoenaed the neighbor's home security video tapes, they may have been able to identify the white truck and white Toyota SUV that were both reportedly parked in their driveway in the days right after the family had disappeared. One neighbor told me that he had seen a "white truck with business letters on the side" parked in their driveway on Monday and Tuesday, February 8 and 9. Was this Mike's truck? When I showed him a picture of Mike's work truck, the neighbor could not say with any certainty that it was the truck he had seen.

The Invisible Isuzu Trooper

The McStays' white Isuzu Trooper was towed from a parking lot in a strip mall on the US-Mexico border at 11:05 p.m. on Monday, February 8, four days after the family disappeared. We know this because the records from the towing company confirm it.

This is all we know.

What we don't know is how long the Trooper had actually been parked there, why it was parked in that particular lot, or who parked it.

Law enforcement has apparently concurred with the parking lot security guards who claim the SUV was parked in their lot at "around 5:30 p.m." that afternoon and then cited as an abandoned vehicle at 11:05 p.m. that Monday night. Security has claimed that vehicles left after dark are towed each evening. This scenario would mean that the McStays left their Fallbrook home at 7:47 p.m. on Thursday and vanished for four days, only to resurface on Monday night.

Investigators cite these four days as crucial to solving the mystery of their disappearance, and they wonder aloud what the family did during this timeframe.

However, I spoke with another security guard there who told me that vehicles are not towed from that parking lot each evening as had been claimed. "Sometimes they are here a few days," he told me.

It is possible then that the Trooper was parked at the lot on the weekend, possibly even on Friday morning. There is no security footage showing the exact time the Trooper was parked at the lot.

The missing four days may not be missing at all. To base any investigation on these four days is without merit. However, for the sake of discussion, let's assume the Trooper was parked there on Monday.

During this ninety-six-hour period, all communication with the McStays abruptly ceased. Their cell phones had been turned off on Thursday night, with all calls going directly to voice mail after that time. There was no bank activity from the McStays during this time, although we have seen that a former business associate transferred thousands from Joseph's account after the first few days of the disappearance. No credit card transactions, no sightings by any friends or family, and no surveillance camera footage that has ever surfaced of the family during this time.

A look at the parking lot pictures reveal that the Trooper was parked in just about the only space at the entire mall where there would be no video surveillance footage. Because of this blind spot, authorities claim that no one saw the Trooper being parked there at 5:30 p.m. on Monday. Was this space deliberately chosen?

I believe that the reason there is no video evidence of the car being parked there on Monday is because it wasn't parked there on Monday at all.

I believe this for two reasons:

First, the security guards who were interviewed had no idea when the car was parked there because their shifts started at odd times, and there were no attendants on duty. In fact, no one actually even remembered the Trooper arriving at the lot on Monday in the first place. Had the Trooper really been parked there by five thirty as some security guards claim, there would have most likely been footage of the family in the next hour and a half at any of the fifteen retail stores in and around the mall. All these retail outlets have video surveillance.

The family would not have been sitting under a tree at a picnic table waiting to cross for one main reason: they had Gianni and little Joseph with them, and it was rainy and at 42 degrees at five thirty on February 8.

Second is the choice of this particular parking lot. This parking lot is known to locals as a "dumping lot," and it may not have been chosen by accident.

When I first drove to this lot to interview business owners in the mall and surrounding area, I was surprised at how perilous the lot was. This was the last place I would park if I had two kids in the car, and it was certainly no place I would ever park after dark, even if alone.

To get to this lot, the driver had to first pass a well-lit parking lot with an attendant and security cameras, which they did.

This cheesy strip mall parking lot has no video cameras, no attendants, and sparse security. The mall includes a liquor store, a Chinese buffet, a food stamps outlet, a Mexican bank, and a military recruiter. At the other end of the mall, about three hundred yards from where the Trooper was parked, is a Ross Department Store. All of the mall's stores have video surveillance, and at least four of them told me that they were never interviewed by law enforcement.

Across the street from this strip mall is the massive outlet mall, Plaza las Americas. This is where everyone shops, and no video footage of the McStays was ever searched for or found from any outlet stores.

But what about the famous border-crossing video that shows the McStays crossing into Mexico?

As we will examine in the next chapter, this video shows what some have claimed is the McStay family crossing into Mexico at 7:00 p.m., roughly two hours after they claim the Trooper was parked. The video was discovered by one of the many volunteers from the National Center for Missing and Exploited Children who had scanned thousands of people crossing into Mexico that afternoon and evening.

I don't believe this video is the Mcstays. I believe that if they did indeed cross into Mexico, it was on Friday, February 5, not Monday night at 7:00 p.m.

The volunteers at the NCMEC were only told to review video from Monday, February 8, not the prior four days.

This explains why no video footage of the Trooper or the McStays was ever discovered on the border or at any of the many retail outlets with security cameras.

They were searching on the wrong day.

Had videos from Thursday night through Monday morning been examined, who knows what we might have learned. The Border Patrol keeps this type of video footage no longer than ninety days, and most business security systems are on a loop that erases after a week or so. Any video footage that could have helped solve this mystery is long gone.

The questions now begin to mount: Why did the sheriff's department not instruct the volunteers to search back to the night of February 4? Why did they not speak to each and every business owner in both malls? Did they already know something that the family did not?

The Video Seen Round the World

There remains only one real constant concerning the mysterious disappearance of the McStay family: from the day the warrants were served by the San Diego sheriff's department on Friday, February 19, law enforcement believed that Joseph and his family had voluntarily left. While there was an outside chance a crime was committed, the most obvious explanation was that they just disappeared on their own.

It appears that law enforcement was also becoming skeptical of Joseph's brother, Mike, and his ever-changing story. What was he not telling law enforcement about his brother's disappearance?

From the moment he reported his brother and family as missing on February 15, 2010, his story began to fall apart. Was it a back window he broke in, or a side window, or an unlocked window as he told us on our radio talk show? Or was it an open door as he told someone else? Did law enforcement tell him he could take Joseph's computers because he was "the brother and could do whatever he wanted" as he proclaimed, or did he know in advance he had taken evidence from a crime scene and faced arrest if not returned immediately, as he was told later by law enforcement?

Why would Mike withdraw $5,000 from Joseph's account if he knew that his brother would be back? Why did he register an FBN under earthinspiriedproducts.com in March of 2010, just a month after the disappearance?

Law enforcement was aware of these facts, but I wonder if Mike's possession of Joseph's computer altered the outcome of the investigation and made it appear to law enforcement that the family voluntarily disappeared, as they originally believed. Unfortunately, as the months have multiplied and law enforcement today may have a different view of this case, mistakes in the early days of their disappearance cannot be reversed.

One of the biggest snafus concerns the famous border-crossing tape that many have suggested is the McStay family.

When the San Diego sheriff's department was told that the McStays' Trooper had been found near the Mexican border, I believe that they already had questions about the disappearance, whether it was voluntary or not, based on Mike McStay's behavior. The fact that the SUV was found three hundred feet from the Mexican border in the California town of San Ysidro probably only confirmed their suspicions.

They were initially told that the Trooper was parked in the strip mall parking lot between 5:00 p.m. and 5:30 p.m. on Monday, February 8, 2010. It was towed at 11:05 p.m. that same night and classified as an abandoned vehicle.

The sheriff's department then decided to search all border-crossing tapes using a twenty-four-hour window, from Sunday night through late Monday evening.

There are upward of 180,000 people who cross at that point every day, so this was no doubt a daunting task. The sheriff's department asked the National Center for Missing and Exploited Children to assist in the search by enlisting volunteers to watch all the videotapes from that crossing, specifically looking for a family of four.

In hindsight, the volunteers should have been asked to search from 10:00 p.m. on Thursday night, February 4, through the 11:00 p.m. hour on Monday night, February 8. But hindsight is always perfect vision.

Tens of thousands of people were observed walking across to Mexico on these tapes. Individuals, couples, big and small families. The only family that seemed to fit the McStays was flagged and has now become the "video seen round the world."

Is the family in this video the McStays? I do not believe it is.

According to Mike, it may be Gianni and little Joseph, but the couple doesn't look like Joseph or Summer. This fits with one of his theories that the kids were taken for the "sex trade business" with the parents being murdered. He told the *North County Times* on February 24 that he "felt in his heart they were taken for sex trade."

Video experts have reviewed this tape, and none can say for sure it is the McStays. In fact, most discount it as really a family of five or possibly even six, not four.

Watch the tape closely, and it appears that another person or two comes from the right of the frame just before we lose the family.

This video is not the McStays for one main reason: it is the only video of that particular family that was recorded that evening.

There are no less than nine cameras on the United States side of that border crossing and another four hundred in Tijuana that are linked to an elaborate system that was installed because of the terrible drug-trafficking crimes in that city. These cameras are in high definition and not a grainy, unrecognizable video as in this tape.

With nine different camera angles of this family crossing the border, the only one we see is one that shows the back of their heads.

Were the other angles erased because the McStays are in federal witness protection? It seems likely, that if the federal government erased the McStays from eight other camera angles, they most certainly would have caught this one as well.

It is most likely that the reason we don't see the McStays crossing the border between 5:00 p.m. and 11:00 p.m. on Monday, February 8, 2010, is because they were not there.

While the Border Patrol will not confirm the length of time they file and store border-crossing tape, we have learned from a former Border Patrol agent that it is most likely ninety days, meaning that any video evidence of the McStays crossing the border from Thursday, February 5, through the alleged Monday would have been erased long ago.

The Curious Condition of the House

Joseph and Summer had been looking for a house near the beach for a number of months. They loved living only a block from the waves in San Clemente but realized it was time to invest in a home rather than continue to rent. The timing was right because they were being evicted from their current home in San Clemente.

They quickly learned that homes near the Pacific Ocean in Southern California were out of their price range, so they turned their search inland. Summer was a realtor, and she knew where they could afford to live or not live. They found a home in Fallbrook, a community as laid-back as Joseph's surfer lifestyle, an area surrounded by thousands of avocado trees with a nursery on almost every street corner. It wasn't the beach, but as far as Joseph was concerned, it was close enough. "Highway 76 is right next to our house, and it runs straight into the Oceanside Pier," he once told his dad.

The plan was to remodel the home in the next two or three years and then sell it for a nice profit. Homes in their subdivision sold for over $600,000 just a few years earlier, so their purchase price of about $300,000 was a great deal.

They both knew that one day they would return to the beach, with Joseph wanting to move to Hawaii one day, so the Fallbrook lifestyle would be temporary.

They moved in just before Thanksgiving 2009. With most of their furnishings stored just north in Orange County, they happily lived out of suitcases for the first month or so.

In January 2010, they had the possessions delivered in a portable moving container and unpacked. Still lacking dressers and other necessary furniture, much of their clothing was stacked on the floor of the bedrooms or on hangers.

As most men seem to have their favorite chair, Joseph's was an off-white futon in the living room, strategically placed for the best view of his 42" flat-screen TV.

The location of the house on a quiet cul-de-sac was ideal for the kids. The professionally landscaped front lawn was perfect for Gianni and little Joseph to practice their somersaults.

A spacious backyard with a six-foot wood fence provided adequate privacy and was also just right for Summer's 170-pound guardian angel, Bear. Behind the back fence was about fifty feet of former greenbelt that, for whatever reason, had been let go, turning to weeds. All that remained were the broken sprinkler heads and concrete drainage system.

The neighbors on the cul-de-sac, while friendly, did not go out of their way to meet the McStays. Only four neighbors still lived on the cul-de-sac twenty months later. All four families were still haunted by what may have happened, and all four have their theories.

As one neighbor told me, "First, they moved in, and I saw the kids playing in the front yard with their big dog. Then a POD showed up, they emptied it, and it was gone. Then the next thing I knew, they were gone. They seemed like a really nice family, and I'm sure they are all right today, probably living in Mexico," he said.

Another neighbor told me that they think it was a craigslist killer. "So many bad things have happened to people when they buy merchandise on that website," she said. "I think someone killed the whole family."

A third neighbor blames the large population of illegal immigrants that allegedly lived in the greenbelt area behind the McStays' house, though no illegal encampments were ever discovered in that area. I walked the greenbelt for a mile or so and did not see even one "illegal."

The fourth family believes that the McStays are in witness protection. "I investigated the disappearance, and I'm sure they are being protected by the government," the father told me. "I have a family member in federal law enforcement, and he looked into the disappearance for me. He assured me they are safe and being protected." When I quizzed him for any kind of evidence supporting this claim, he said that his family member could not divulge anything but that "they were safe."

When the McStays allegedly drove out of their driveway at 7:48 p.m. on February 4, 2010, they would leave behind a house that was their unfinished dream, or at least Joseph's dream. New granite countertops, new appliances, and new wood floor were about to be installed.

Aside from the obvious remodeling going on inside, the condition of the house had been an unanswered question in this mystery.

When sheriff's deputies walked the house on Monday, February 15, they noted that a carton of eggs as well as Summer's prescription eyeglasses had been left on the kitchen counter. They also said that dirty diapers had been left throughout the house.

Yet when McGyver had been at the house just two days later on Wednesday night, there were no eggs on the counter or any eyeglasses. "I didn't see any of those items on February 17," said McGyver. "The kitchen counter had just been cleaned by Susan, who kept mumbling to herself something about protecting Joseph's older son." What could she have meant?

The dirty diapers are curious as well, according to her sister.

"Summer was never known as a neat freak housekeeper, but she certainly wasn't the 'chronically messy wife' who forced her family to live in squalor, leaving dirty diapers all over the house," Summer's sister, once told me.

"She had placed many of their belongings in plastic bins that were stored in the garage and was very well organized," said Summer's sister Tracy.

What about the soiled diapers that were allegedly left all over the house? "Her house was always clean and tidy," says her sister. "She would never just leave dirty diapers lying around. She would always put them in the trash container in the garage. If there were soiled diapers on the floors when the police examined the house on February 19, they weren't put there by my sister or her family."

This statement appears to be inconsistent with her statement about the condition of the house when she and her mom toured it at the end of February. We also know from e-mails that Summer had chastised her brother for telling her to clean up her dirty house, which was the reason they were being evicted from their San Clemente apartment.

Where then did the dirty diapers come from? It is possible that someone may have removed the dirty diapers from trash containers in the garage and placed them on the floor in the house, but why?

Had the house been staged for the sheriff's deputies? Why was Susan so hurriedly cleaning the kitchen when McGyver arrived at the house on Wednesday night, February 17? Why was she even in the house in the first place when it had been declared a crime scene on Monday, February 15?

Perhaps more curious is why the sheriff's department failed to fingerprint the house. If they had, whose fingerprints might have been found on the egg carton, Summer's glasses, or the dirty diapers?

The Mexico Sightings

The McStay family had been missing for about a month when the sightings began. Predictably, the family was first "seen" in Mexico. The famous border video that allegedly showed the four crossing into Tijuana from San Ysidro, coupled with law enforcement's belief that the McStays had voluntarily disappeared, made this Latin American country an expected hotbed of sightings.

When a missing person, or in this case, a missing family, is "seen" by one or more witnesses, it is critical to determine whether or not the sighting is credible.

Was the eyewitness account based on only pictures from a missing person's flier? Was the eyewitness absolutely convinced of their sighting? How close was the witness to the suspected missing person?

The distance between the witness and subject is most important in determining credibility.

In his 2005 article in the Journal *Psychonomic Bulletin & Review* (vol. 12, no. 1, pages 43–65), Geoffrey Loftus examines the importance of this distance:

"At 10 feet, you might be able to see individual eyelashes on a person's face," he says. "But at 200 feet, you would not even be able to see a person's eyes. At 500 feet, you could see the person's head but just one big blur. There is equivalence between size and blurriness—by making something smaller you lose the fine details. As a face moves further away, its details become progressively courser and more difficult to recognize."

Another important factor in determining the credibility of any sighting is the number of people involved. Was the subject seen by just one witness, or were there many? Obviously, the more the better, but even with many witnesses, the sighting may still be open to skepticism.

The Daniel Wilson case is a prime example of why sightings of missing persons by multiple witnesses may still be unreliable.

In August 1988, Daniel Wilson abruptly left his home in Washington State after being given a few days off from work for fighting with coworkers. It is now believed that he may have been suffering from carbon monoxide poisoning, which made him act so belligerent toward his coworkers. This conclusion was drawn after his car was examined and was found to have had a major exhaust leak.

At any rate, he left his home and headed to Colorado to visit family, or at least this was assumed. He never showed up.

His car was found on the side of the road in rural Montana, and there was no sign of him—no sign of a struggle, nothing. He had just vanished. His mother immediately began a search, and numerous people came forward claiming that Daniel had been staying at a homeless shelter in a small Montana town. The mother went to the shelter and interviewed the witnesses who all were "positive" that they had met Daniel. She looked at the shelter's logbook, where she saw the name Daniel Wilson. She compared the signature to her son's own handwriting signature samples. It was a match, or so she thought.

However, a short time later, Daniel's body was found about five miles from his car. He had likely died of exposure to the elements after leaving his car.

Does this mean that because his body was found relatively close to his car that the homeless shelter staff and others who claimed to have seen him were simply mistaken? The authorities believed so and discounted the sighting. But could the authorities have been wrong?

Consider this scenario: It is a fact that the homeless shelter where Daniel was allegedly spotted was in the town closest to where his car was found. Let's say that Daniel's car stalled or he just pulled off the road because he was feeling ill from the carbon monoxide leak. He heads back to the last town he saw and ended up at the homeless shelter where he signed in, ate dinner, and rested for a bit. He then returns to his car, which still would not start, and eventually wanders off into the desert, where he ultimately dies from exposure.

In this scenario, the eyewitness accounts and the signature in the homeless shelter's logbook that was verified by his mother were both accurate even though discounted by the authorities.

Granted, had there been video proof of Daniel's presence in the town or at the homeless shelter, this scenario would have become fact. One of the disadvantages to living in a society where video surveillance and DNA science is used as never before in history is that many valid eyewitness accounts may be discounted unless they are supported by this new high-tech standard.

The following three Mexico sightings have all been dismissed by law enforcement for various reasons. However, our investigation has revealed that at least one sighting was most likely Joseph and his family.

The first lead that placed Joseph or his family in Mexico was uncovered by a private investigator in the second month of their disappearance. James Spring, a San Diego investigator who has spent hundreds of hours in Mexico looking for missing persons, believed that the family might have headed down to the Baja Peninsula because of Joseph's love for surfing.

When Spring arrived at the tiny town of El Rosario, he found a possible clue: a signature in a motel registry that might have been Joseph's.

This tiny town is located about two hundred miles south of Tijuana, where the family allegedly crossed into Mexico. It boasts 1,700 residents, has four motels, and is famous for Mama Espinoza's lobster burritos. The area is also a popular surfing spot, which could certainly attract Joseph. I found many online posts about the surfing there and how to find the best spots. Here is one:

> As you enter El Rosario, make a right at the first Mercado, then make left at first dirt road, go over a stream, (there is a make shift bridge) then proceed west. When you reach the village keep going west until you see a radar tower on hill, you will see a sign that says Punta Baja. Make left and always keep towards the right. As you arrive to the beach you should be south of the point. This is perfect camp set up. On the cliffs there is a stairway down to beach. There is a guy named Carlos, he lives at the point and he loves to trade his ocean catches for your beer. The water is cold and the winds kick in pretty hard, so have warm clothes for night. Good luck surfing!

When searching the registry for a small motel often used by American surfers, Spring discovered that a man had registered for a room under the name of Bryan Joseph on March 26, 2010. It was the spelling of the name *Bryan* that piqued Spring's attention as this is the exact spelling of Joseph's middle name.

"I spoke with all of the maids and workers at the motel, and not a single person remembered seeing the children, both of whom I believe would have stuck out dramatically at this place," said Spring.

However, a waiter at a restaurant near the motel specifically remembered a family of four, two young boys and their parents. He noticed that the parents were looking at a map, which they mistakenly left behind on his table. The waiter then put the map in the office, ready to return it when the parents returned for it. Sometime later, he noticed a flier for the missing McStay family and wondered if it had been that family at his table that day.

When Spring happened upon the restaurant with pictures of the McStays, the waiter told him about the map.

Spring turned the map over to the FBI, who checked it for fingerprints. Joseph's and Summer's fingerprints were on file, a State of California requirement as they were both licensed realtors. It appears that authorities do not have Gianni or little Joseph's fingerprints on file because they never fingerprinted the Fallbrook home.

Was Bryan Joseph really Joseph McStay? If so, where were Summer and the kids? Because there were no eyewitnesses to the family and no one could identify ever actually seeing the Bryan Joseph who had signed the motel register, this lead was dismissed as "unconfirmed." Fingerprints later confirmed that the map belonged to a Canadian family.

However, there was another lead that pointed to Joseph being in the same area just a few months later.

This lead came to the McStay family website, www.mcstayfamily.com, in the form of an e-mail.

Jim, an American who was living in Cabo San Lucas at the time, claimed to have seen Joseph in June 2010, over four months after he disappeared with his family.

"I may have seen Joseph at Walmart in Cabo San Lucas today," wrote the eyewitness. "It was around noon, and he was alone. If it was Joseph, it appears he didn't cut his hair. He looks just like the picture in your ad."

The next day, Mike McStay responded to the e-mail, seeking more information.

> This was yesterday? Was he alone? Anything else? If this helps to locate my bro, sis, and nephews, I will also see to it that you get whatever reward money we can spare. Our family is worried sick about them.

Jim then gave Mike all the details leading up to the possible sighting:

> Mike I live off grid and do not have a US phone. I am doing this from an Internet cafe in Todos Santos. I was reading the Gringo Gazette at breakfast yesterday and saw the ad. About one hour later I was shopping at the Wal-Mart in Cabo and this guy pushes a cart by me. His picture was still pretty fresh in my mind. I have lived down here 4 1/2 years and have seen first hand how people on the run end up in this area. If there is any way I can help just ask. Not sure what else I can tell you, Jim.

I contacted Jim, and he told me that no one had ever contacted him after his e-mail conversation with Mike.

"I'm not like 100 positive positive it was Joey," he told me, "but it sure looked like him."

It did appear odd to me that Jim was now referring to Joseph as "Joey" when his earlier correspondence from June 2010 had never used the nickname. Had he met Joseph? Had they become surfing friends?

Joseph and Summer's Fallbrook home.

Aerial view of their subdivision

Still shot from border crossing video

Summer, without glasses

Summer

Summer and Joseph McStay

Summer and Joseph. What is Summer thinking?

Summer citation for leaving Gianni in car unattended

On the kitchen counter is the vase that Summer's
mother said was thrown in the trash and broken
by Mike's mom. The base is cracked in two
places. The granite countertops are in place.

Summer's vase with broken base.

Joseph's futon with the cover missing.
The cover has never been found.

A nice desk, an empty toolbox. The drawers were
still full of empy file folders, pens and paperclips.

Toys, some new but all in great
condition in the boys' room.

Joseph and Summer's clothes, one new pair of
jeans, in a corner of the master bedroom.

Front room of McStay house.

Bedroom.

Mother and Brother Plunder

Joseph and his family had been gone for about five months when his mother and brother did something that is difficult to understand. They looted his possessions.

It was the first week of July 2010. Joseph's mom, Susan, had just called Summer's sister Tracy to let her know that she and Mike were headed over to Joseph's house. She told Tracy that she and her mom were welcome to meet them there as well. What Tracy and her mother saw once they arrived at the house still haunts them to this day.

"We originally went to the house the end of February 2010, and now we were back five months later. Let me describe the difference between the two visits," said Tracy. "In February, about two weeks after they vanished, everything was already rummaged through, and the kitchen was clean. The only things neatly in order were Summer's fake furs from the thrift store. A wedding dress, her nighties, and some high heels were on display.

"Everything else was in a mess piled in their master closet. All the bedding had been removed from the air mattresses. They had the two Little Tikes playhouses in the house and one in the backyard. One was at the top of the stairs with a dog carrier and another playhouse in the master bedroom.

"There were dirty diapers left throughout. The trash cans on the side of the house were full of tons of paperwork with trash stacked on the lids.

"The window in the kitchen was not broken. There was a futon couch without the cover [the cover is in the Christmas pictures] in the family room and a dining room table with a chest, a fake tree, an umbrella holder, wiring, remotes, and a flat-screen TV on the wall.

"There was new wood flooring in the living room piled ready to be installed and a huge throw rug rolled up. There was also a big conference room–type table in there.

"They had linen in the linen closet, and in the master bath, everything was a mess and had been gone through. Downstairs in the office was a desk, a computer. In the closet there were a few baby clothes hanging and stacked on a bookshelf.

"The downstairs restroom had a ceramic setting that had been broken and trash on the floor. The pantry and refrigerator-freezer were stocked with food and alcohol. Cupboards stocked with pots, pans, utensils, and dishes. There was an espresso maker on the counter.

"The bedroom closest to the master merely had another Little Tikes playhouse. The kids' playroom had a little table, books, and tons of toys. The bathroom upstairs had a stone stepping rug that still had the tag on it and was meant for an entry door, not a bathroom.

"On the side of the house were the vanity tops for what appeared to be the upstairs bathrooms. The shed was pretty much empty but looked like it had been rummaged through. There was also a playhouse in the yard and an outside shower that they had at the beach house connected up against the house.

"There were planters and tons of plants. Inside the front door was a pair of Uggs that they claim Summer was wearing in the famous border-crossing video as well as a pair of one of the boys' shoes.

"The garage was full of Joey's tools, crates of baby stuff, baking equipment, six or seven surfboards, three or four bikes, a crib, three strollers, water systems, a Shop-Vac, and tons of miscellaneous stuff.

"That was the condition of the house and its contents the end of February 2010," concluded Tracy.

When Tracy and her mom returned to the house in July five months later, it had been stripped.

"We arrived at the house to find that Mike and a friend of his had stripped the house clean. They had apparently started their removal of Joey's and Summer's possessions the day before.

"The flat-screen TVs, no major appliances. All of Joey's surfboards were gone. The expensive wood flooring was gone. Only one bike was left. All of Joey's tools were being loaded onto his friend's truck, and the place was an absolute mess," said Tracy.

According to Tracy, Susan would then do something so hurtful, so reprehensible, that it would put Summer's mother in the hospital.

"Susan began to throw away Summer's personal property," said Tracy. "I just couldn't believe it. My mom was hysterical and asked her to stop. Susan just looked at her and said, 'Summer won't need this where she is.'

"My mother broke down as she watched Susan throw into the trash one of Summer's favorite flower vases, a beautiful orchid piece. She begged her to stop and removed it from the trash." (I found this vase as I toured the house, the base broken.)

Then according to Tracy and her mother, Susan began to throw away many of Gianni and little Joseph's clothes.

"I couldn't stop her," said Summer's mom, "so I just began to pray that God would stop her. My Summer had only been missing a short time, and it was as if Susan was trying to remove any memory of my daughter from her own home."

Tracy told me that she contacted the sheriff's department to report that Mike and Susan had "stolen all of Joseph's valuables" and was told that only Joseph could file charges.

"What a slap in the face that was," said Tracy. "The sheriff's department wouldn't even do the humane thing by asking Susan and Mike why they had stolen Joseph's stuff."

What did Susan and Mike do with all of Joseph's valuables? They have claimed it was to pay back child support to Joseph's son from his first marriage.

However, neither Mike nor Susan have ever told Tracy or her mother what was sold, for how much, and where all the money went. Many of the possessions they took and sold did not belong only to Joseph. They were Summer's too.

Why did Susan, in the midst of throwing away Summer's personal possessions, tell Tracy and her mom that "Summer won't need this where she is"?

Did Mike and Susan know that Joseph wasn't coming back?

The Threat:
"Muzzle Your Wife"

Joseph met his first wife at a Southern California church in 1990, and they were married two years later. In 1997, they had a son. In early 2000, their marriage seemed to waver, at least in the mind of his wife, who was beginning to set her eyes on other men, one man in particular.

Joseph's wife was working for her father, a wealthy man who owned a jewelry store in Southern California. While working in the sales department, she met the wholesale jewelry salesmen.

She could have had no idea what effect meeting this man would have on her marriage and the life of her son or her husband, Joseph.

In late 2000 or early 2001, Joseph's wife began to spend more and more time with this man. Their relationship turned sexual, and soon she was pregnant.

When Joseph learned of the affair and pregnancy, he was devastated, according to his father. "I spent hours on the phone with Joseph during this time," said Patrick. "He was a broken man over this whole thing."

According to Patrick, Joseph even offered to raise the child fathered by the jewelry salesman if she would end the affair and attend marriage counseling with him.

"She agreed when he made that offer," said Patrick. "My son must have truly loved her if he was willing to raise that child as his own." However, after agreeing to end the affair, she failed to do so.

A short time later, they agreed to divorce, and the marriage was over. But while his marriage may have ended, the consequences of his wife's affair with this man would follow Joseph until the day he vanished.

Soon after the divorce, his ex-wife and the jewelry salesman married.

Enter another man into the life of Joseph's firstborn.

"Joseph was very concerned that this man would ultimately hurt his son. He knew how violent this man was toward women and was afraid his son would be victimized," Joseph's father, Patrick, told me.

Joseph seemed content with the custody arrangement for his son that included Wednesday nights and every other weekend. His ex-wife was very open to their son spending more time with his dad. Joseph rarely went to her house to pick him up. She would either drop him off at Joseph's house, or they would meet somewhere for the exchange.

Through the years, Joseph had maintained a good relationship with his ex-wife right up until his disappearance on February 4, 2010. In fact, she would often head to Joseph and Summer's house seeking counsel for various situations, a habit that apparently infuriated Summer.

Summer had told her sister Tracy about a number of times when the ex-wife would show up at their house unannounced to talk to Joseph. "Summer was upset that the ex-wife would just walk in to the front door of their home to find Joseph. A couple of times he was in the shower, so she walked right in to talk to him," said Tracy.

Patrick believes that the stepfather had a violent past. While I did uncover a police record (with prison time served) for a man with the same exact name as the stepfather, I cannot definitively prove they are one in the same, so all references to his violent past are speculation.

It does not appear the stepfather and Joseph ever clashed with the parenting time arrangement.

However, that all changed during the summer of 2009, when something happened with Joseph's firstborn.

Joseph and Summer had met with his son to talk about alleged abuse in July of that year. Both took extensive notes. Two videotapes related to this alleged abuse were recorded and secured by Joseph and Summer and given to a trusted third party to hold in case anything happened to them. They remain secure today.

Summer then filed an official complaint with California Protection Services for an incident that was related to their conversation with Joseph's son.

It appears to me that this complaint was all part of the strategy devised by Summer a few years earlier. She wanted Joseph's relationship with his son to end, I believe. While she may have pitched this to Joseph in a way that made it appear she really wanted Joseph's son to live with them, I believe she had ulterior motives.

The strategy of the false abuse charges backfired.

"Either you muzzle your wife, or I'll come over there and kick your ass and muzzle her for you," was the threat Joseph received in a phone call from the stepfather, according to Patrick, who had talked at length to Joseph about the threat. This all occurred during the time of the CPS investigation.

"It was apparent that Joseph had serious concerns about this man and knew of his violent past," said Patrick. "Joseph took the threat very seriously and felt as if his and Summer's lives were in danger."

Summer had also told her sister Tracy about the threat and repeated it to her verbatim. "She didn't like backing down, but this man scared her to death," said Tracy.

Why would the stepfather allegedly issue such a serious threat? Patrick believes that it is because of this man's criminal record. Again, I cannot confirm that the stepfather is indeed the man Patrick believes him to be, and I trust that law enforcement has already gone down that road.

Another reason why he may have responded as he did was because the charges were false, all of them, and the complaint that Summer made to CPS was false as well. I have been on the receiving end of false charges, and while I did not respond with threats as this man allegedly did, it certainly did cross my mind.

Joseph was also afraid of the man, and Summer now realized that she had not thought this strategy completely through. She was now in over her head.

Patrick told me that another threat Joseph had received was that "once the CPS investigation was complete, that false charges would be leveled against Summer as an abuser of her children, with the goal being her kids' removal from their home."

Were they getting ready to run?

According to an email Susan Blake sent Joseph after their disappearance, the investigation was closed the first week of February 2010. Here is the email where Joseph's mother refers to the CPS investigation:

> The case was dropped and he is cleared. The State is not at all involved nor is the counselor. It was over in January.
>
> So no matter who tells you anything I will swear it is dissolved and closed. The FBI know this, police etc.
>
> So if you ran because you thought the State was taking your Sons, it is a LIE a sick LIE. Not true & Summer will do anything to get everyone out of your life. She has problems Joey and it has messed up your life and everyone elses."

I did make numerous attempts to interview the stepfather for this chapter in order to present his side of these events, but each time he refused.

Did the stepfather carry through with his alleged threat of "muzzling" both Joseph and Summer by murdering the entire family as some claim? Did Joseph and Summer have an unannounced plan to keep their family safe in the event they lost the investigation?

Old Boyfriends
Never Die

When I began my research for this book, many believed that Summer's ex-boyfriend, Vick Johansen, had something to do with the disappearance.

Not true, and here's why:

Vick never stopped loving her. Here is an e-mail he sent Summer in September of 2005:

> Summer, I am sincerely happy for you and your family. I am proud of you.
>
> I assure you I am a true friend of your family. You can still call me if you ever need help with anything. Dont forget about me, I am still out here. I genuinely care about your well being, and all those that you love.
>
> Friendship can be the most beautiful of true love. The trials of life will always reveal the truth.
>
> I believe in you Summer. Don't forget. I truly believe in you. Knowing you're out there gives

me faith in the world. Knowing that you are blessed with a child shows me that you're beauty is blossoming into the world.

All of my heart goes out to you. Summer Girl Forever.

That is not a message from a jealous ex-boyfriend as many have claimed. These are words from a man who still loves his ex.

I can find nothing that would place suspicion on Vick here, but plenty that might incriminate Summer in the way she began her relationship with Joseph.

Let's go back to May of 2005 and review an e-mail that Joseph sent to Summer. She is six to seven months pregnant, still living with Vick, and dating Joseph, apparently in secret. It appears from Joseph's message here that Vick might have asked Summer about Joseph. We know that Vick and Summer were selling the house, and part of this message is about the listing. However, Summer was still living with Vick and seeing Joseph. In fact, it appears that Summer did not begin to live with Joseph until after Gianni was born.

From Joseph:

Yes...he has to understand that...and u r 2 big!...You both must leave Sun. night...You are coming down the hill to work and stay with Stein and Bill doing loans and notary.

You met me through McGyver and My dad is helping financially to help you keep the property and sell it so it doesn't get foreclosed on, so he [Vick] can get some money and go to Hawaii or whatever.

You can go to my moms...gate code: ****, garage code ***enter...Your in! He must understand that no one including you can be there while the house is listed. It is time to be professional and time is of the essense. And...I miss you & little one terribly and I worry when he's around...soo much...

Summer had claimed to her sister, mother, and others that Vick was abusive to her. That he had "beaten" her, locked her out of the house in Big Bear, forcing her to endure subfreezing temperatures all night.

I do not believe this. I have not found one shred of evidence to support her claims. and no one has ever been able to provide any when I have asked for it.

There is another twist that involves Vick and Summer.

We know that Summer was two months pregnant in January 2005, which would mean conception was November 2004. Was Joseph secretly seeing Summer in the fall of that year? Yes, he was. Here is an e-mail conversation between the two in July and August of 2004:

From: summergrl@hotmail.com

To: josephmcstay69@hotmail.com

Date: Thu, 29 Jul 2004 15:03:35 -0700

Thanks for the quick fix.

Hope all is well with U. I can't answer the phone so you'll have to leave a message if U want me to hear your voice. If U miss me, why didn't U give me a hug or kiss goodbye? U would'nt even lend me your CD, remember? Thats no way to show someone U care. I guess, it is fitting all things considered.

Have Fun in the Water. May all your Days be Bright!

Me

Here is Joseph's reply to Summer's e-mail:

U R Sooo....Funny... Where do you come up with this stuff? 1 I told you, I would burn u a copy of the CD and send it. 2 I felt very uncomfortable being on your street, at your house where u live with your boyfriend who is sick and waiting for you...It wasn't the time or place...U know I can't keep my hands off u otherwise...3 It sucks...to have to lie, hide, can't even call freely, can't even be ourselves...ow well... I have done a lot for you...How can u focus on the mundane and not the significant things these past 3-4 weeks...hopefully you were joking...lol... Ciao. Joseph

This proves that Joseph was dating Summer in August of 2004. It also shows that Vick did not know and that Joseph did not like lying about it.

Further, we don't know why Summer or Joseph did not claim Gianni on their Federal income tax returns.

Was Vick Gianni's biological father? Did Summer know this? Did Joseph know this?

Not proof that Vick is Gianni's biological dad, but odd just the same.

This we know: Joseph loved Gianni. Everyone knew this, and the YouTube videos prove it. If Joseph had any doubts about Gianni's biological dad, it didn't matter. Gianni was his son, and Joseph was a loving and caring father.

Then, two days before Christmas 2009, Vick sent Summer this e-mail:

> I love you for ever...Happy Birthday Summer... for ever and ever... -Vick

I made numerous attempts to talk to Vick in 2012 both via e-mail and cell phone, with no success.

The Spider Weaves His Tangled Web

There is little doubt that Joseph surrounded himself with some less-than-desirable characters, ex-cons and others who might be described in much the same way Clint Eastwood described himself in *Unforgiven*: "a man of notoriously vicious and intemperate disposition."

One such dubious character might be Dan Kavanaugh, Joseph's former webmaster.

Throughout this mystery, Dan has remained at the top of the list of possible suspects, or at the very least, knowing more about the disappearance than he has admitted.

I began emailing Dan in October 2012 with questions related to Joseph's finances; specifically a number of PayPal transfers that he had made into his own personal account after Joseph had disappeared.

He answered my emails but not my questions, so in November, I asked him to call me so we could chat, and to my surprise, he did.

He wanted me to believe that he wasn't too concerned about the case, calling it an "old case that no one cares about anymore," but I sensed this was not the way he really felt.

I told him that until he answered the many questions about his actions in the days and weeks after the disappearance, he would always be seen as culpable in the disappearance.

"I will let the people on the Internet think what they want, they are all their own Starsky and Hutches and it doesn't bother me to hear their amateur conclusions. I don't spend any time reading it, and have my own life to worry about," he told me.

During one of our phone conversations toward the end of November, he asked me about writing his own book, a "Tell-All," as he called it. His book would "set the record straight about his relationship with Joseph.

I asked him for some examples of what would be in his book.

"I will detail how Mike called EIP clients after Joey's disappearance and told them to send their checks directly to him and not the company," he said. "He made a lot of money off his missing brother in February and March, 2010. One client sent him $15,000." (We also know from Joseph's PayPal records that Mike transferred $5,000 to his account on March 26.)

I offered to help him write this book and put him in touch with my publisher. On November 26, he emailed me the table of contents for his prospective book. Here are the chapter titles:

I was most interested in his theory that Joseph was killed over a deal gone bad, but when I asked him to tell me more about it, he resisted. When I pressed him for the name of the bad client it became clear that his theory wasn't viable. He didn't know of any particular client, just figured one could have been bad. This "deal gone bad" theory had floated on the Internet for years, never with any credible evidence to back it.

His book idea began to fade however, when I explained to him that it needed to include his answers to the many questions about his actions concerning this case. I provided him this list of questions:

1. How did you gain access to Joseph's PayPal account to begin to transfer money to your personal account?

2. Was it you or Mike who ordered a the new copy of Quickbooks on February 8 and why?

3. Who initiated all the money transfers from Joseph's bank accounts to his PayPal account?

4. Why did you update Joseph's mailing address for his Wells Fargo account on February 12? If it wasn't you, was it Mike?

5. Where did all the PayPal money transferred into your account go?

6. What was the $2,700 cashier's check for?

7. What was the $10,000 check for?

8. Why did you have EIP clients send money to your grandfather's Paypal account?

9. Did you have a legal right to sell EIP?

10. On March 16, Mike registered EarthInspiredProducts.com. Was this so you two could sell his company?

11. How much did you sell EIP for?

12. How were you able to sell EIP when you were not the owner?

13. Where did the proceeds for the company go?

14. Did you claim all this income on your federal taxes?

Dan Kavanaugh stopped calling me when I pressed him for answers to these questions. Last I heard, he was going to self-publish his tell-all book so that he could finally "set the record straight." He never answered any of these pertinent questions.

It is hard to figure out Joseph's relationship with Dan. Was he just the webmaster or was he a business associate as he told me? Did Joseph entrust Dan with the PayPal account password or did Dan hack into the account to transfer thousands of dollars into his personal account? Some of these answers can only come from Joseph, because Dan is not talking. What is certain is that there was time in 2009 when Joseph had become alarmed of Dan's behavior.

Here is an e-mail that Joseph sent to an employee at the domain company that hosted his EIP website. It took place a year before his disappearance.

> Hello Paul,
>
> Thanks for taking my call. I really do appreciate it.
>
> First of all I want to thank you for all of your efforts in keeping EIP ranked these past years and as of recently, allowing us to pay late, reduced amount, etc. I really do appreciate it. It's nice to know there are those out there who genuinely want to help others be successful.
>
> As you are well aware, it's been extremely difficult these past months due to I think primarily this dismal economy and we do sell a "luxury item" which is the 1st to go when people are simply trying to survive and only buy necessities. We haven't formally met... I simply pay you folks each month these past years. I

allowed Dan to deal with you since he is the SEO specialist for the site....

As of recently, due to the declining sales, etc., Dan Kavanaugh and myself have been having a "falling out." To give you some history: We met around 2001 when he helped build our Electronics Website and we became friends.

He is extremely talented, but young. So, from time to time he'd need $$$, I'd give it to him and he'd give me software, etc. He was just a kid at 21-22 back then. He didn't have a car, so I let him use a Volks Vanagon I wasn't using to help him out.

I've been doing building fountains since 1998 and originally built earthinspiredproducts.com in 2000. I'm passionate about fountains. I built them & love them. It's not just for $$$ for me. The site didn't do much till 2005 when I got together with Dan & suggested we revamp EIP from the dead and give it a go. Then 1,000's of hours redesigning began, re-establishing relationships with past vendors, etc. A lot of late nights & coffee among other things.

Since then with your help, PPC, etc. we've built it up pretty good. Yet 2008 was tough at times and extremely difficult this past 3 months in particular.

I'm 39 years old, have a wife & 3 kids. Dan is 28, single, no kids. Very few responsibilities & parties like a rock star, heck can't blame him.

But, the success of eip is much more critical to me than to him. I can't couch hop as he could, I have mouths to feed. I know from experience, that you "have to save up for the rainy day" and I did now for 4 yrs. Dan never did.

Whether he made $3,000 or $8,000 in a month, it was gone as soon as he got it.

I was raised by a single Mom who was like a father & mom to me, strong & solid w/ a good work ethic, Dan didn't have that luxury. It was difficult for him, thus it's made him who he is, Abandonment issues, Lack of Trust, etc.

Having said all the above, Dan has become quite malicious towards me to the point of affecting my family. Please see IM string below.

It's quite sad, since we considered him like family, w/ my 2 youngest calling him "uncle Dan." I would appreciate your input and any help you could recommend.

Fountains are my life, EIP feeds my family. I can't have EIP disappear off the face of the earth and end up back in a cubicle working for someone else. But, if I have to for me and my family to survive, I will.

I do wish the best for Dan. I will not be malicious as he is being. And perhaps we can work through this or part ways amicably, I don't know.

Either way, I wanted to give you folks a "heads
up" on the situation. I appreciate your help.

I guess my first question after reading this email
would be why would Joseph continue to use this man
as his webmaster when he had become "malicious"
toward him?

But, it is clear from Joseph's PayPal records that he
did just that, continuing to pay Dan right up until he
vanished. From what we can see in the records, probably
$800 per month to maintain the EIP website.

If that email isn't revealing enough, Joseph also
included a recent IM conversation he had with Dan
that seems to reveal his malicious side:

Joseph:	What?
Dan:	ill speak with u on the phone or something
Dan:	dont im me, unless you want to talk about some s***
Dan:	like i said tho, if u try and postpone handling this because u don't like confrontation, it wont be to ur benefit, but live the dream lol
Dan:	it will be about 30 days from today that your site is gone from the search engines if u just wanna ignore me
Joseph:	And why is that?
Dan:	why not, u treat me like a kid like im dumb or some s***, your site will be gone from the engines, i will make my own fountain site.

Dan: so get it out of your head that i cant do anything. i made an offer to let u have the site and buy me out. u fumbled that one

Joseph: Now, I, Summer & Kids know the "Real You" and what you would potentially do to harm me and my family. Your a great guy Dan. **** Sad.

Dan: dont try your guilt trip shit on me bro. you and i had a business. do what u want man. i wish the best to u and ur fam. but dont burn fools.

Joseph: Yay right... do you see the "contradiction"... You wish the best for me & my family, but have no problem destroying our livelihood? Your sick or something?

Dan: ive told u the options, you choose what's best for you. you can disreguard my offer to buy me out and continue thinking your site is permanent, or you can simply do it, and keep your site. *and i wont do anything to harm* ill give u ppc access to my s*** and everything and keep ur links up not pointing to my new fountain site and you can keep the site that isnt even that good, like u said yourself.

Joseph: Your a great guy Dan. At least we all know your true colors.

Dan: be more legit in ur future biz ops, with partners and you might go far.

Dan: we had a good thing goin for a while apparently its not worth salvaging though to you. i gave u chances

Dan: no worries, better luck on ur next one, but u wont get another me, and there's lots of you.

Dan: your lazy, smart, but lazy, thats why you never built any other sites like mine

Joseph: What do you want Dan?

Dan: i want to be treated fairly, and more respected as a owner of this business not simply some kid you throw a bone to once in a while

Joseph: Even if we came to a $$$ amount and you were paid...Given the malicious things you have written above, you would take the $$$ and still do those malicious things. What's the point? There is no reasoning with you or fairness with someone like you.

Dan: here's the deal, ill give u a gentlemans promise since were bros for years and i dont hate you we just had a falling out were buddies u think i want to **** with u like that. Wrong. ill respect your site *and your future with ur family* and even help u with the site still that i havent pulled any of ur links youll rank for years when things bounce back youll do well.

Dan: or, whatever u want man, point is ill honor our deal if u buy me out nothing malicious of any kind will be done its an offer on the table a legit one. ill give you a day to come up with what you wanna do, and get back to me with a dollar amount thats fair, and we'll get past this, it was nothing

Dan: we dont have to end this badly, and you dont have to buy me out all up front. you can make payments, we can work something out, so you can stay afloat. but without me, the site will die, and it took 4 years to get it where it is. hit me up tomorrow and let me know what u decide. sleep on it, whats that site worth to you. and your future. cuz i can make more

Dan: youd be pretty screwed, and im not ****** around

Dan: so now that you know how serious i am, and what im capable of you can make a better decision how to end this

There are least five personal threats issued from Dan to Joseph in this instant message thread, yet, Joseph continued to use him as his webmaster.

Immediately after Joseph's disappearance, Dan began withdrawing large sums of money from Joseph's PayPal account. He obviously had obtained Joseph's password for the account. Did Joseph give it to him or did he obtain it illegally?

On Saturday, February 6, 2010, Dan initiated a transfer of $2,000 from Joseph's PayPal account into his account.

On Monday, February 15, 2010, Dan transferred $3,000 from Joseph's PayPal account into his account. This was four days before the authorities would show up at Joseph's house with the search warrant.

On Thursday, February 18, 2010, Dan transferred another $2,000 from Joseph's PayPal account into his account. This was just one day before authorities would head to Joseph's house with their search warrant.

Did Dan know that Joseph had gone missing? According to an e-mail he sent to Summer on February 10, he knew something was up:

> Dear Summer,
>
> Where is Joe? He was supposed to send me $800 on Saturday and his phone has been off and not accepting more messages. Is he in the hospital or something? I'm sincerely worried for him.
>
> Let me know asap
>
> Thanks! Dan

According to this e-mail, Joseph was supposed to send Dan $800 on Saturday, February 10, and he makes it appear that he never received the money. Yet we know from PayPal records that Dan had already transferred $2,000 into his account on the tenth.

The withdrawals continued. On February 24, Dan transferred another $2,000 into his account:

Your payment has been sent

2/24/10 To Earth Inspired Products

From: service@paypal.com (service@paypal.com)

Your payment for $2,000.00 USD to daniel.kavanaugh@xxxxxxx.xxx has been sent.

Amount: $2,000.00 USD

Transaction Date: Feb 24, 2010

Transaction ID: 97L9863056536422W

Then another $3,000 to Dan on March 11, 2010:

Your payment for $3,000.00 USD to daniel.kavanaugh@xxxxxxx.xxx has been sent.

Payment details

Amount: $3,000.00 USD

Transaction Date: Mar 11, 2010

Transaction ID: 8YC86879M69289114

Dan had now transferred into his own account $12,000 in the thirty days since the disappearance.

There is another unsettling e-mail sent from Dan exactly one month after the disappearance to a prospective client. It appears to show that Dan was misrepresenting himself and Joseph's company by giving this prospective client his middle name:

> From: Eip Fountains [mailto:eipwallfountains@ yahoo.com]
>
> Sent: Thursday, March 04, 2010 4:11 PM
>
> To: Seaman, Mike
>
> Subject: Re: Depaul Water Feature
>
> Dear Mike,
>
> My name is Vince, I will be able to handle everything for you as Joseph is away out of town. Please call me on my cell at 858 717 ****
> or e-mail me back.
>
> Best Regards,
>
> Vince Kavanaugh, EIP Water Features

I was unable to contact this individual to learn more about this possible transaction.

Dan was quick to accuse Mike McStay of intercepting client's payments to EIP after Joseph's disappearance, but it appears he might have been doing the same thing.

Here's a copy of a Better Business Bureau complaint filed by a former client who had ordered a fountain in August 2010:

Complaint: 02/05/2011: Ordered the product on 08/30/2010, they sent me an email with payment instructions. The instructions were to send the money via PayPal to johnpughley@xxxxxxx.xxx. I called the company to MAKE SURE the payment was to be sent to the email address listed on the invoice and was told. YES. He was the owner's father and that was how it needed to be paid for. I have copies of the invoice (showing payment instructions), and a copy of my PayPal receipt showing funds were sent as prescribed.

Why would Dan instruct this EIP client to transfer money into his father's PayPal account?

The Friend Who
Lost The Most

Of all of Joseph's friends or business associates there is one man who I believe lost the most when Joseph disappeared.

Chase Merritt.

He was the last of Joseph's friends or family (that we know of) to lay eyes on him on February 4 and he was the last person Joseph would call that evening before his cell phone battery would eventually die.

He doesn't know what happened to his friend. He never did, even though law enforcement believed he knew something.

"The detective kept telling me that I had to know something and he asked me to take a lie detector test," he said. "I talked to my attorney who recommended that I not take the test and so I called the detective back and told him no."

However, after talking to the detective for some time on the phone, he changed his mind and agreed to the test.

"I had nothing to hide and so I agreed, but I told them they needed to meet at my attorney's office and conduct the test there," he said.

Two detectives and two test personnel met him at his attorney's office where he took the test.

He passed.

"No one told me there that I had passed, in fact they wanted to say that there were 'inconsistencies,' which I knew was not true. I heard later that I had passed."

I asked him if Mike had taken the test.

"I understand that they asked Mike to take a lie detector test and he refused."

On a typical day, Chase and Joseph would talk on the phone four or five times. On February 4, they had met for lunch to talk about an order for a fountain in Saudi Arabia. After their meeting, Joseph headed south to Fallbrook and he headed to his home. That afternoon they talked two or three more times while they were on the road. By early evening, he had returned home and had talked to Joseph who was back in the Fallbrook area.

At 8:48pm his cell phone rang.

"It was on his kitchen counter and I looked at who was calling. It was Joseph. I didn't answer it because we had been talking all day and I needed to spend time with my wife. I just thought I'd call him back the next morning."

Joseph didn't leave a message and he never called Chase, or anyone that we know of, again.

"Obviously, now I wish I had answered his call," he said.

He would return Joseph's call on Friday morning.

"There was no answer so I left a voicemail," he said.

He called a number of times on Friday and all throughout the weekend of February 6, still with no answer.

On Monday, February 8, he drove to Joseph's house because he knew something wasn't right.

"We talked many times daily on the phone and now I couldn't get a hold of him at all for four days, so I thought I'd just drive down there."

On his way to Joseph's house, he stopped by Joseph's mother's house. He asked her if she had heard from her son in the past few days.

"She looked at her phone and realized she hadn't heard from him since Thursday the week before, so I drove on to the house," he said.

He didn't go in the house but walked around back and found the dogs there. He fed the dogs with food he knew was in the storage shed and left the shed door ajar so the dogs would have cover.

"It had been a rainy few days and there was no place for them to find cover but in the shed."

Chase had a profitable partnership with Joseph in the fountain business.

Joseph would take the fountain order from a client and he would design and build the fountain. He would then take pictures of the fountain, send to the client and with approval install the water feature if necessary.

"Joseph would ask for a fifty percent deposit with the order and the rest was paid before we shipped or installed the fountain," he said.

"After Joseph disappeared, I had a few fountains that we were working on that needed to be completed. I finished all those fountains but didn't help Dan or Mike with the ones they were selling after the disappearance."

He told me that he had a dozen phone calls from clients who had paid the fifty percent deposit for a fountain and were concerned because they had not heard back from EIP.

"Dan and Mike were selling fountains and taking all these deposits and not designing or installing fountains. I had a bunch of calls from these clients who had paid their deposits and never received their fountain. One call was from someone who had ordered a $25,000 fountain from Dan," he said.

After he had completed the fountains he and Joseph had started, he went to Saudi Arabia to install the $80,000 masterpiece that had been the topic of their lunch meeting on February 4. Following that trip, he was finished with EIP. He didn't appreciate the direction the company had taken after Joseph's disappearance and wanted to distance himself from Dan and Mike.

"I was never paid for the remaining fountains I completed after the disappearance and wanted to protect my reputation. I suppose I spent $15,000 of my money to complete the orders that Joseph and I had together, but it was worth it. I had to do the right thing," he said.

In the months after Joseph's disappearance, EIP's company rating went from A+ to F. Complaint after complaint came from clients who had paid their deposit but never received their fountain. Here are just two:

May 5, 2010

Complaint: I ordered a water feature in March. I have been calling and emailing to check the status of the order for about 3 weeks. No one will return my call. I have still not received the $899 water feature that I ordered. When I tried to pay with a credit card on the website I got an error that said something about it being "unsecure"; therefore I called the company. The company requested that I pay by check.

Business Response: The card was never charged, please call direct at 858 717 xxxx. Our site now has a security certificate, but had a brief day or 2 with the SSL being down, that is why you got the error. Please call and we will help you Thanks Eip

Consumer Rebuttal: Your company requested I pay by check. I overnighted the check to expedite the process. Our check has CLEARED. We have NOT received the water feature AND no one has returned my calls or emails for four weeks. Because of your company's failure to reply to me and your lack of customer service DO NOT SEND THE WATER FEATURE I ORDERED FROM YOUR COMPANY. YOUR COMPANY NEEDS TO REFUND ME $899 IMMEDIATELY. Your website advertises a money-back guarantee—I trust that you will honor your company's advertising.

August 30, 2010

Complaint: Ordered the product on 08/30/2010, they sent me an email with payment instructions. The instructions were to send the money via PayPal to johnpughley@xxxxxxx.xxx. I called the company to MAKE SURE the payment was to be sent to the email address listed on the invoice and was told. YES. He was the owner's father and that was how it needed to be paid for. I have copies of the invoice (showing payment instructions), and a copy of my PayPal receipt showing funds were sent as prescribed.

I asked Dan Kavanaugh why he had clients make deposits to his father's PayPal account, but he never answered.

I could tell from my conversation with Chase that he was sad the company was so thoroughly destroyed in just a few months. He knew there was nothing he could do but walk away.

He has remained quiet throughout this mystery, proving his friendship to his missing friend. He has been offered as much as $20,000 to tell his story but has steadfastly refused. I don't know why he talked to me, but I'm glad he did.

Following the disappearance, he immediately lost his income and his personal as well as physical life took a turn for the worse.

Today, he has recovered and is continuing his entrepreneurial ways of making money and living the American dream. In fact, I suppose I helped him in a small way by purchasing one of his newest, exclusive products.

I have learned that this man is the kind of guy who subscribes to the code that views any disclosure of information about a friend, whether good or bad, to be a form of snitching. This is exactly why Joseph knew he could trust him.

Summer and Her Loan Modification Scam

According to an AskMen.com report in 2012, the top five unethical jobs in the United States are pharmaceutical company director, conflict diamond dealer, tobacco marketer, car salesman, and porn site operator.

The report states that these are "the lowest worms on the food chain and thrive in an immoral, unethical profession that feeds off the 99 percent."

I believe that there is another profession in the United States today that is lower than any of these previously named five: loan modification broker.

This nasty occupation makes these other guys look like sweet Sunday school teachers in comparison, and this was one occupation that Summer was heavily involved with.

Driven by money and a low moral compass, these players seek out homeowners who are behind on their mortgage payments, promising to save their homes from foreclosure by getting the homeowner's loan modified.

Homeowners typically are required to pay $6,000–$10,000 in advance but often fail to enjoy any of the advertised benefits and still lose their home in the process.

The tactics used to sell these loan modification services first became the focus of criticism in the media and elsewhere in the wake of the housing collapse in 2006, and by 2010, the Federal Trade Commission responded to growing reports of abuse by implementing the Mortgage Assistance Relief Services rule.

Known as MARS, it bans these maggots—mortgage brokers, lead generators, and affiliated marketing companies—from collecting "advance fees" from homeowners. Instead, loan modification firms are permitted to collect fees only after homeowners have received written loan modification offers that they deem acceptable from lenders or servicers.

One of the most revolting loan modification companies was Home Rescue Programs of Marina del Rey, California, a company that Summer represented.

Summer owned a rescue-your-house-loan-modification site, which she registered in September 2008. The Internet address was www.rescue-your-house.net. We have the complete set of screenshots from this defunct website.

Brian R. Suder was the president and founder of Home Rescue Programs. According to his LinkedIn profile, Suder was "a tenured real estate and mortgage expert who was mentored for more than two years by one of the nation's leading experts in the loan modification industry, a former Commissioner of HUD. To date, Brian has helped thousands of homeowners save their homes from foreclosure through successful loan modifications."

However, Brian Robert Suder was banned from offering loan modification services in Washington State in 2010 after doing business without a mortgage broker's license.

He was fined $12,000 and had to refund $9,195 in fees collected from at least four consumers, according to an order from the state's Department of Financial Institutions.

Brian Robert Suder was also banned from engaging in loan modification services in Maryland in 2009 over a failure to obtain the required license, according to an order from the state's Commissioner of Financial Regulation. He and four others were fined and ordered to refund more than "$55,000 to at least 20 homeowners for failing to obtain loan modifications for them," the order states.

Summer's e-mails reveal that she began communicating with Suder in January of 2009, and it appears they were quickly on a first-name basis.

From: Summer Martelli

Date: Tue, Jan 20, 2009 at 10:16 AM

Subject: Loan Modification

To: bsuder@xxxxxxx.xxx, Brian Suder-Home Rescue

Hi Brian, Hope this finds you in good spirits. As for us we are getting better coming to grips with some tragic family news. I've been dealing with my cousin (22yrs old) and told she is terminal(maybe 3months left) as you can imagine my focus has been with her my mom and aunt. Although, we are pulling thru its been challenging.

I'm now starting to focus on work and had a few questions for you regarding load mods. I spoke with a lady who is self employed and whose income has dropped drastically. She has been using her Credit Cards to help make up the difference in income loss. She currently has not missed any payments but knows she will very soon. The property has equity ($95K) She does not want to sell.

Also has $60K in Credit Card debt. What I was wondering is if the Bank would consider lowering payments from $2600 to perhaps $1200 even just temporarily and perhaps using her equity has a bit of security? Does this make sense? Can you do anything for her? Let me know what you think.

Best Regards, Summer & family

Mr. Suder replied two days later:

Subject: Re: Loan Mod.
From: briansuder@xxxxxxx.xxx
To: summergrl@xxxxxxx.xxx
On Thu, Jan 22, 2009 at 11:29 AM
Call me, 949-637-xxxx
Brian Suder-Home Rescue

It also appears from Summer's e-mails that she was learning to operate the low-moral compass necessary to be successful in the loan modification business. What is interesting in this next e-mail is that Summer no longer signs her name as "Summer and family" but as "Me." Certainly not a professional signature by any means. Had she spent time talking with Suder on the phone? Had she actually met with him, or was she just one of his hundreds of independent contractors?

On Thu, Jan 22, 2009 at 11:29 AM, Summer Martelli wrote:

Greetings Brian, Thanks for the continued support much appreciated. I need your advice, I have an account that wants to sign up with us. They are generating approx. 400 leads per week via radio ads they are currently sending them thru an Attorney Co. and are being paid $1k. per deal. They clearly want to make more money.

Now, I've been talking with them for some time now and have been very selective in the information I have shared in that I've given the impression that we are selective in who we will accept as clients thus making them Want to work with us. I want to sign them up but I want you to convey the same message.

This company is also doing credit repair and according to Jeff we are too, so you may want to keep that in mind as well. The last time we spoke I believe you said, I would be paid $300 per deal is that still accurate? As of today they are sending me five deals. Please send me your thoughts.

Best Regards, Me

There is no response from Mr. Suder, so Summer sends him another message the next day:

On Fri, Jan 23, 2009 at 12:54 PM, Summer Martelli wrote:

> Greetings Brian, I've tried to phone you but I realize you're very busy. I just finished the web call with Sara and she was able to answer a few questions I had infact i will be phoning her shortly. I hope your well and look forward to speaking with you soon.
>
> Best Regards, Summer.

Mr. Suder replies three days later:

> To Summer Martelli
>
> From:Brian Suder (briansuder@xxxxxxx.xxx)
>
> Sent:Mon 1/26/09 10:21 AM
>
> To: Summer Martelli (summergrl@hotmail.com)
>
> Thank you Summer.... Welcome to our team....

We learn from screenshots on Summer's website that she actively pursued building her business the rest of 2009, at least until November, when everything started to fall apart.

Here is an advertisement she ran on her website seeking clients:

> I am a DRE BROKER and after many months I have finally received an APPROVAL for

my ADVANCE FEE AGREEMENT. I am consulting with brokers that wish to be 100% compliant with the state loan modification laws. It is a great business that can earn you a lot of revenue however you should do it the right way because there are a lot of regulatory agencies cracking down on noncompliant brokers/companies.

The law states that you cannot accept an advance fee for a loan modification, unless you are an attorney or have a DRE approved Advance Fee Agreement.

Most Brokers take months and spend thousands of dollars to get an agreement approved with the DRE because of all of the revisions.

If you are interested in doing loan modifications properly and want to have a correct agreement to submit to the DRE, please e-mail your name, position with the company and contact info and I will contact you.

I will provide written approval from the DRE of the Advance fee agreement and required accounting paperwork to become approved right away. I will give you the exact packet I sent in so that you can get approved with 10 days as well. E-mail me @ advancefeeagreement@xxxxxxx.xxx.

How much money was Summer making? This statement sent to her from Home Rescue Programs headquarters gives us some idea of her potential:

Home Rescue Programs LLC we receive anywhere between 15-45 files per day. Our company is experiencing INCREDIBLE growth and is nearing 350,000 of gross sales PER MONTH and looks like it will continue to grow each month by 50% easily!

We have no idea how many loan modification clients Summer was able to secure for Suder in 2009 or if the two of them ever communicated outside of e-mail. But it is obvious that it was just a matter of time before the authorities would catch up with Suder and his loan modification scam.

Following are policy changes sent to Summer by the company's headquarters. They show the dubious and illegal nature of the business:

We need everyone to follow the instructions below and "Destroy" any old contracts and please replace them with the attachments to this e-mail. THIS IS YOUR RESPONSIBILITY and we will not coddle ANYONE.

Changes:

· Florida is now included with California, Illinois, Maryland, Colorado and Washington.....please update your contracts!

· ALL deals need to be pre-approved by using the Pre-Qual sheet included with this e-mail. YOU MUST ENTER YOUR FULL NAME AND CONTACT NUMBER ON THIS FORM.

· Full payment is to be remitted with "Full Package" to... Home Rescue Programs LLC 1329 Clipper Heights Avenue Baltimore MD 21211

· If you are closing 3+++ or more deals per week and or, you live on the West Coast please touch base with our administrators at admin@ xxxxxxx.xxx we will provide to you our DHL account number for FREE to ensure proper delivery of your deal.

Direct Deposit is now available!

Contracts & Payments:

All deals are to be 100% complete with ALL supporting documents and FULL payment to:

Home Rescue Programs LLC not Richman and Associates!

There are absolutely NO exceptions to this rule. If you have a verbal agreement with Brian Suder or Brookes Bruno to except full payment and only remit our fixed cost this document will over-ride any of these verbal agreements and will be in effect starting Tuesday August 26th 2008 so you have plenty of time to get this right with any outstanding documents that you have currently in circulation.

Unless you have written permission from our Administration Staff Members

If you need to send us additional documents on a file and or, the borrow wants to give you "New" documents that they have received from there lender please do not e-mail or fax Brian or Brookes. The procedure in affect as of Tuesday 05, 2008 will be for you to fax additional forms with a fax cover page with your client's name and phone numbers and your contact information to.

~FAX NUMBER ~ 323-255-xxxx~

Underwriting for an Approval and Processing the File / Week 1 and 2:

Once we receive a file, it is held for a 3 day right of rescission and then underwritten. Once the file is approved, it is sent to our processing department.

In Processing 3 Distinct Things Happen.

1. The authorization to represent is sent out to the lender(s)

2. The client is e-mailed their username and password for the client status website.

3. If there is any outstanding paperwork, the client will get a call from processing requesting that paperwork.

Bank Appointed Negotiator / Weeks 3 to 5:

From there, the file is assigned to an underwriter/negotiator from our firm. Our underwriter/negotiator can easily wait a month before the lender acknowledges receipt of the authorization and appoints their own negotiator. (Loss mitigation departments are extremely backed up in today's market – Many lenders and service providers are rehiring underwriters as negotiators to catch up to the volume). Until a bank appointed negotiator is assigned, we are at a holding pattern. Your clients need to aware of that in the beginning stages because there will be a lack of communication during this time. We can NOT coddle the client, what we need to do is "Negotiate" in the most aggressive manner in behalf of clients that have retained our service. PLEASE SET THE RIGHT EXPECTATIONS this is also an excellent time for you to build referrals and it's also why the "bulk" of the commission goes to YOU.

***Once the lender appoints their negotiator, your client will get a call from their Richman appointed underwriter/negotiator. ***

Negotiations 1 Month:

Communication between our underwriter and your clients will pick up here. The underwriter will then package a complex and detailed report to the lender. The negotiation process can take up to an additional month. The process is kind of a secret but very effective. The client then receives a new payment that they can afford and the modification is complete.

Total Time Frame 2 months 3 weeks

(We are the best at what we do. If there is a lack of communication at the beginning stages it is because we are waiting on the lender to appoint a negotiator. Once we build momentum, we will be in contact with your clients on a regular basis.

Your client will not be making their mortgage payment during this time. This will free up some cash for them for when the negotiations are done.

This process is not easy for your clients. Many of them will be an emotional wreck. They will need you to set the right expectations and assure them they are in good hands.)

It was just a matter of time before it would all hit the fan. In November 2009, Summer received this e-mail from her team leader in Arizona:

From: Melissa (melissa@xxxxxxx.xxx)

Sent: Thu 11/19/10 6:46 PM

Hey Team! I'm not really sure where to start on this e-mail. I got word TODAY that Home Rescue Programs has closed its doors. This is not a hoax. I'm not sure what it means for all of us who have files in at this time.

Summer would learn the damage:

Date: Wed, 27 Jan 2010 12:26:15 -0700

Subject: Hi

From: melissa@xxxxxxx.xxx

To: summergrl@hotmail.com

It is my understanding that Brian moved down the street and opened up another shop. CRAZY! We estimate he abandoned over 2000 files. The DRE is actively investigating Brian and Steven. I heard they subpoenaed their bank records. That can't be good. Also...I heard they took in multiple files after shutting their doors, losing their broker of record and declaring themselves out of business. They cashed the checks and did nothing with the files. I believe that falls under the FRAUD category. YIKES!

I have not sent any files to UMS and at this point I don't plan on using them. I'm actually moving away from mods in the traditional sense. They just don't seem to solve the REAL problem for my clients.

That problem being for most of Arizona, the clients are SUPER upside down on the home. So great...you get a reduced payment, but you still owe $200,000 more than the home is worth. These people end up walking eventually. So, i'm working with a Short Pay Refi team and a Note Buying team. That seems to be working well for me and my clients. What have you been up to?

Melissa

We see from this next e-mail, sent the same day, that Summer was concerned about going to jail:

OMG, that is so crazy! I have a hard time understanding how people think they are gonna get away with this. The thought of going to jail keeps me from any kind of crazy thoughts!! I've been hearing a lot bad stuff but it's hard to know what is true and what is talk, ya know?

As for me I gave a call to UMS but got a bad vibe so I passed them up. Most of my clients need to sell or surrender the property so I reactivated my RE.Lic. so I can list as short-sales. Although, I think a Short-Pay Refi. would be the better choice. I just don't any info or contacts on that, maybe you can fill me in.

My husband tells me to quit all together and be his "wife" but I really enjoy helping people not to mention making my own money. If you have any suggestions send me your thoughts..I appreciate your update, I'm still in shock over Brian and Steve. wow!

Summer

One would think that if Summer was concerned about going to jail that she at least thought she had committed a crime.

Also, I wonder what "crazy thoughts" Summer was having? Were any about disappearing?

Another revealing statement here is when she writes that Joseph wants her to "quit and be his wife," she was obviously spending a lot of time on this business.

We have no records detailing how much money she was actually making or if Joseph even knew what her income had been. She may have been direct-depositing all her funds into her North Carolina Credit Union account, an account we have never been able to locate but we know existed when Summer wrote of it in e-mails to her brother. Here is the e-mail:

From: Summer Martelli

Sent: Jul 11, 2006 3:13 PM

To:

Subject: RE: hello your very happy bro

Good, I'm glad your stoked. My account is in North Carolina so it won't be done until the morrow but it will done. I'll e-mail you when its confirmed. Now, please what about that letter from sister?

On Thursday, January 28, just one week before Summer would disappear, she had an e-mail conversation with her team leader in Arizona, trying to find a way around complying with California real estate law:

On Thu, Jan 28, 2010 at 2:24 PM

Summer Martelli wrote:

So, I meant to ask you this yesterday but I was so shocked by Brian & Steven that I forgot!! How you guys getting around the DRE Lic. needed to neg. on loans on Short-

Pay Refis? That's been the huge hurdle over here, ya know

Thanks, Me

Date: Thu, 28 Jan 2010 15:40:33 -0700

Subject: Re: Hi

From: melissa@xxxxxxx.xxx

To: summergrl@hotmail.com

The DRE License? Or the SB94? I'm not working in California is I guess how I'm getting around it! LOL! I know different companies have different strategies for side stepping SB94. None of them really make me feel very good. Per SB94 you are permitted to charge a REASONABLE sign up fee upfront. Less than $500 seems reasonable to most. The rest of the money is either paid at the back end OR if its recommended, the client pays $995 for a forensic audit. That is a tangible service. That doesn't happen upfront and a different company is doing the audit. Its all very interesting...

SB94 was written for the banks...by the banks. The people getting hurt the most are the homeowners.

Melissa

The very next day, with Suder's Rescue Your House business being shuttered and Suder himself now heading to indictments by the Maryland Commissioner of Financial Regulation and the Departments of Real

Estate in California and Washington, Summer's team leader sends her a final e-mail:

> We are moving the offices, let the negotiator staff go and are sub contracting the existing modifications out—the gov't is making it nearly impossible to do mods with getting the money in advance and most states are following CA's lead.

> The Internet is down and the phones are off–so I don't know if anyone will get back to you or not but I am sure we will all find out what is going on next week. HRP is going away, but we will reopen as a Forensic Audit Company with mods on the back end and the Capital Mitigation for commercial mods.

> I have been talking to another modification company in California that is trying to build a model to help with your current files. We have not figured if out completely, but if you have URGENT files, I suggest you get in touch with Don Hubbard of United Mortgage Solutions. His phone number is 888-880-xxxx.

> Let him know you worked with HRP and Melissa said to call. Again, I don't know to what extent his company can help, but Don is a stand-up guy and their approach to modifications seems to extremely successful.

> Depending on when you turned in a Forensic Audit, HRP was forwarding those Audits to Peter at Equity Credit Options.

Please contact Peter via e-mail (peter@xxxxxxx.
xxx) to find out if they have your audit and what
the status is. Their website is: http://xxxxxxx.
xxx/contacts.php.

I'm doing my best to get answer and find
solutions for us. At this point I have ZERO
trust or faith in Brian Suder and Steven
Duplain. I suggest we all prepare for the worst
and be pleasantly surprised if they do the right
thing and complete the mods they have started.
Per David via Susan, it looks like we won't
know much until early next week. I will keep
everyone informed if I hear something.

For now, here is alternate contact information I
have for people:

Brian Suder: Cell phone–949-637-xxxx /
Personal E-mail–briansuder@xxxxxxx.xxx

Steve Duplain: Cell phone–310-902-xxxx

Susan Herman (Broker of Record): Personal
E-mail loangoddessinc@xxxxxxx.xxx

So far the HRP websites and e-mail address
seem to be functioning. I don't know how long
they will be up.

Sorry for the bad news.

Melissa

I spoke to Melissa in November 2012 and asked her
about Summer as well as her time at HRP.

She claimed, "Summer was on a distribution list for HRP. When HRP started going down, I made it my mission to notify as many people as possible that they should *stop* sending files to HRP. HRP gave me the bulk of the agents that I worked with. And if you're familiar with the rule of 5%, you'll know that 95% of the work was done by 5% of my agents. Therefore, 95% of my agents were just taking up space on an e-mail list.

"ALL of my *personal* clients did get their mods. One of them even got a sizable reduction on their second mortgage with Litton in addition to saving money on their payment. This is why I believed in HRP. When things started to get shaky, I stopped submitting personal files, and when things imploded, I let everyone possible know.

"Brian and Stephen were so shady at the end, they even cashed checks that they received the day they shut the door."

Melissa claimed that she didn't know how many open files Summer had at this point, which was the end of January 2010.

I had a good friend who went through this loan mod process in 2009. He had never been late on any mortgage payment in the preceding six years. Now, in a bad economy, he signed up with an agent from HRP, paid his $3,500, and trusted the agent that his mortgage payment would be reduced from $9,000 a month to $4,000 per month. He had only wanted to reduce his payment and keep his credit FICO score at 850.

Months went by with no word on the status of the payment reduction. During these months, he was instructed by the loan modification company to "stop making his monthly payments" and "just wait for the new reduced payment." After six months, his agent would not return his calls; in fact, her voice mail remained full so he could not even leave a message.

Finally, his house went into foreclosure, and his credit rating had dropped from a perfect FICO score of 850 to less than 700 in less than a year because he had not made a mortgage payment for over six months.

I remember well how frustrated he became when the agents would not return his phone calls about the status of the modification. He had paid his $3,500 and was now waiting for a reduced mortgage payment. It never came.

I helped him move from his house and out of state. His final words to me were "I should have killed that loan mod b**** for what she did to me."

Did Summer take money from the wrong person? Was she threatened by this client once they learned that they had been duped?

Six days after she received this e-mail from her team leader, Summer McStay and her family drove away from their home, leaving everything behind.

A Bizarre Twist with Brian Robert Suder

While this may have nothing to do with Summer, it is nonetheless intriguing. Brian Robert Suder was arrested on February 2, 2012, just two days before Summer and her family disappeared. But he wasn't arrested for loan modification fraud as one might think.

We read in *People v. Suder No. G043409* that a "jury convicted defendant Brian Robert Suder of stalking [Pen. Code, § 646.9, subd. (a)], making a criminal threat [Pen. Code, § 422], and simple assault [Pen. Code, § 240]. The court suspended imposition of a sentence and placed defendant on five years' probation with the condition he serve 365 days in jail. Various fees and fines were also assessed. A ten-year no-contact order was issued, and defendant was also required to attend Batterers and other programs."

According to court documents, here is what happened:

> Defendant and F.V. dated for not quite two years, living together for part of that time, before she began dating Joe Wooten. Thereafter defendant tried to convince F.V. to get back together with him.

> One night, when F.V. was sleeping, defendant entered the bedroom of her residence without her permission. She awoke to find him lying on top of her, holding her arms above her head.

> He proceeded to take off his shirt and scream at her about dating someone else; F.V. was afraid. After she was able to convince him to go to the living room, they argued and he pushed her to the couch. Police ultimately took defendant from the house.

The next day defendant sent text messages to F.V. that he was going to her workplace and that he was in her bedroom; he stated he would "take care of" her roommate if the latter did anything.

Defendant sent hundreds of text messages to F.V. alternately professing his love and hate, stating he wanted to kill her. He also called F.V. at work 20 to 30 times a day. As a result she did not perform well at work and was terminated. Although F.V. told defendant to stop he refused.

After a short respite, defendant resumed his calls and texts to F.V., which sometimes reached 200 per day. His threats became more violent, including stabbing and killing her, and telling her of connections with the mob, who could make her disappear. Defendant's conduct scared F.V.

Was Mr. Suder falsely accused by his ex-girlfriend, as is sometimes the case? Mr. Suder apparently appealed his conviction. According to www.leagle.com, here is the final appellate opinion:

> *Defendant was given 30 days to file written argument in his own behalf. That period has passed and we have received no communication from him. We examined the entire record to determine if any arguable issues were present, including those suggested by counsel and found none.*

So if Brian Robert Suder was innocent of these charges, he apparently wasn't concerned enough to defend himself, and his conviction was upheld.

Where Is Brian Robert Suder Today?

Isn't it fascinating how people with no scruples—or, more to the point, dirt bags—always seem to pop up somewhere else after they have been outed?

"The Litigation Compliance Law Center works only with mortgage professionals dealing with repercussions of MARS, and they've been able to transition their offices over," Brian Suder told his webinar audience.

"We offer a much better product, more aggressive, with an aggressive stand against the lender. We want people who already have existing mortgage companies. It's a product in which a lot of people were doing mods [mortgage modifications] and veered away from that because of the legal repercussions."

Suder continued hawking his new product: "Seventy-five percent of all mortgages qualify for mortgage litigation. Mortgage brokers can easily and quickly create a pipeline of 100 clients a month."

Suder continued, "You go ahead and you sell the retainer, which is typically $5,000, and we pay each broker for their [sic] expertise. This is set up so each mortgage company or marketing firm can market this product and we take over from there. Your clients get a phone call from an attorney prior to selling. It sets up the sale and they [clients] talk to a real attorney. .

The litigating law firm does their [sic] own compliance call to make sure there are no guarantees. You can't make guarantees."

The Litigation Compliance Law Center lists no physical address and Chad T-W Pratt Sr. as its only attorney. Pratt, a 1989 graduate of Loyola Law School, is separately listed as a senior litigation attorney at Real Estate Law Center PC. The Pasadena, California, firm appears to be a one-partner shop, Its letterhead jointly bearing the name of the firm, and Chad T-W Pratt & Associates Inc. lists as its local phone number 441-CHAD.

Confirmed Sightings?

The Walmart in Merida, 2010

Bob Yeater, his wife Tessa, and their three children have served as missionaries in the large Mexican city of Merida for over ten years. Following is their account of meeting Joseph, Summer, Gianni, and little Joseph in April of 2010, more than two months after they had disappeared from their home in Fallbrook, California.

Tessa and her oldest daughter, Amber (not her real name) had just arrived at Walmart to pick up fish and vegetables for that night's dinner. As they entered the store, they passed an American family of four. The two young boys stood out to Amber. "The older boy had this wavy hair and was so cute," she said. "And the younger one had a birthmark on his forehead. I said hi to the boys, and they smiled and looked real happy."

Amber's mom tried to strike a conversation with the mother. "She was cordial, but I could tell didn't really want to talk," said Tessa. "The father never really looked us in the eyes. He always turned away and didn't say much."

As Amber and her mom walked the aisles of the store, they would pass this family twice more, each time with Amber saying hello to the two small boys.

"They were so cute," she remembered.

Again they would see this family as they entered the checkout line to pay for their groceries. "They were right next to us in the next line," recalled Tessa.

When Amber and Tessa left the store, the American family exited at the same time. Amber told the small boys good-bye as their parents were putting them in their car seats in their minivan.

As Amber and Tessa drove away, they both commented on how cute the boys were. "I wonder though why their dad never looked at us," said Amber.

Later that night, Tessa was on the family computer looking at her favorite American website, when up popped an alert for a missing family of four.

She leaped from her chair, ran to find her daughter, and said, "The family we just saw at the store, the one with the cute boys, they are on the computer!"

Amber looked at the alert and agreed. "Without a doubt, that is the McStay family," she told her mom and dad.

Convinced that both his wife and daughter had seen the McStays, Bob sent the tip to www.mcstayfamily.com, the family website. Mike McStay showed no interest in the sighting and e-mailed the lead to his dad, Patrick.

Patrick contacted the husband and asked if there were video cameras at the grocery store. "I am not sure," he told Patrick. "I'll drive to the store now and see."

He contacted Patrick later that evening with the good news that there were cameras in the store and that they should have recorded Joseph and his family. He told Patrick that the store would release the video, but only to the police.

Patrick then contacted the San Diego sheriff's department about the sighting, and Detective Troy Dugal said he would begin the process of acquiring the video.

The FBI was brought in and, along with the Federal Mexican Police, requested the video from the store.

Patrick was told by Detective Dugal that he would be called once the video had arrived.

Weeks passed and no call.

When Patrick phoned the detective, he was told that the first video sent was the wrong one. Once they located the right one, it was sent to a specific agent at the El Centro, California, office of the FBI. By the time the video arrived in El Centro, this agent had been transferred to Washington, DC, just days earlier.

The video was then forwarded to the agent's new office there. He apparently viewed it and sent the video to the FBI special agent in San Diego, who then forwarded it to the San Diego sheriff's department and Detective Dugal.

The detective called Patrick and said the video was "grainy, and no faces could be identified." He told Patrick he would send the video to Amber and Tessa to confirm this was indeed the tape of the correct time and Walmart.

Both Tessa and Amber confirmed that the video was grainy and that they couldn't even tell if it was the same Walmart.

"We know the family we met was the McStays," said Tessa. "Their young son had the birthmark of little Joseph, the older son had the curly locks of Gianni, and Summer was wearing the same glasses as she does in all the pictures. The only difference was that Joseph had a buzz haircut."

"The lack of any video doesn't change who we saw," said Amber. "It was the McStays."

Here is the follow-up e-mail from Bob Yeater that I received just before publication:

> Rick: My wife and daughter were convinced enough to contact total strangers. We weighed the options before making contact. Who wants to make the call as a 'false alarm'?

> We watch TV and never think these things will happen. They simply came home and saw their face on the front of AOL's webpage and my wife called me into the room saying, 'I just saw these people…' She then called in my daughter (who was with her) and pointed to the boys photo and said, 'do you know them?' My then 12 year-old says, 'Yeah, I just saw them at Wal-Mart'.

> Too many things made sense:

> 1. The father was dressed like a casual beach bum/ surfer type.

2. The mom had long, straight, dark hair.

3. The dad had his head shaved.

4. The little boys both had hats on, with a birthmark on the forehead of the youngest.

5. They are in a Wal-Mart that only locals use, no tourists, speaking English.

6. Merida is the safest city in the country.

7. Four-hour drive to English-speaking Belize.

You have to realize, as an American, in a foreign country, ESPECIALLY women and girls, they detect and check-out any American/English speakers. We make many friendships this way and also simple curiosity.

I am no detective, but I am shocked the only thing that was done was a request for grainy video footage from a produce department. Just my opinion though.

They left the store in front of my wife walking by an outside video camera, literally 15 feet from them, with no other people around. Like I said, seems like a blown opportunity. I sent the Detective a copy of the receipt once as they even checked-out at the same time.

Southport,
North Carolina, 2012

Tracy Skehan never forgets a face. She may forget your name, but if she ever meets you, she will never forget your face.

Tracy believes that she met and spoke with the entire McStay family on Tuesday, August 28, 2012, in Southport, North Carolina.

Tracy works in a popular diner in this tourist haven that is located on the coast in southeastern North Carolina where the Cape Fear River meets the Atlantic Ocean.

This undiscovered paradise with a stunning setting on the banks of the infamous river is known for its calming ocean breezes and fully content residents who chose to call this little slice of heaven home.

It is not an easy drive to Southport by car, so many choose to take the thirty-five-minute ferry ride from Wilmington that operates every hour throughout most of the year.

On this Tuesday morning, Tracy was at the front counter of the diner acting as hostess when a family of four walked through the front door. Here is her account:

"I was at work at Local's Family Diner in Southport, North Carolina, when a family came in looking very much like the McStays, though the older child had blond hair.

"They looked so familiar to me, but I just couldn't place them. The man looked like a surfer. He was tan and wearing a surfer necklace, hair kind of long, not shoulder length, but long. He was wearing a funky hat.

"The woman was wearing a hippie dress. It was an embroidered skirt, and I liked it. She was also wearing a floppy hat with sunglasses, and I noticed that she didn't take them off once inside the diner."

Tracy asked them if they wanted a table, and they opted for take-out food.

"I handed them both a to-go menu, and after a few minutes, they placed their order. The man ordered for the older child. I'd say he was about ten. He ordered hash browns, and the boy seemed excited.

"The woman spoke very softly when she ordered, and the man asked her in a nice way to please 'speak more loudly.' She then ordered for the younger child, maybe six or seven, a biscuit and sausage sandwich. I thought it was a bit odd that the woman never looked up. She always looked down and was very soft-spoken.

"The younger child could have been a boy or a girl, I just wasn't sure. The child had a very strange haircut, long bangs that covered the forehead and one eye. I thought it was odd that a young child would have that type of haircut."

After they ordered, Tracy said the woman and the two children went outside and waited by their truck. It was a gray Toyota Tundra.

"They were having fun with each other outside."

The parking lot is small, and Tracy had a clear view of the truck and family.

"The truck had a bike rack on the back with four bikes attached. It wasn't a new truck but was nice and in good shape. There was a lot of stuff in the back of the truck, nothing that stood out to me."

At this point, Tracy was frustrated. She knew these faces but could not place them.

Then it hit her. She had watched a missing persons TV show a couple of months earlier about a family from Southern California who mysteriously disappeared on February 4, 2010. This was that family!

"I couldn't remember the name of the family from the TV show, but I knew their faces. I knew it was them, at least the man and woman anyway. I never forget a face."

Once it hit Tracy that these were the McStays, she struck up a conversation with the man, who was waiting by the counter for his order.

"I engaged in small talk with the man and asked him where they were from. He said, 'We just came through New Jersey.' I thought it strange the way he said that. He didn't say that they lived in New Jersey, but that they just came through there."

The take-out order was ready, and the man headed out the door. Tracy wanted to take a picture of the man and the truck, but the line of diner customers was now long, and she couldn't leave her post. Plus, she had a new cell phone and had not used the camera on it as of yet. She did, however, head over to the main window of

the diner to watch the man get into the truck and drive off, hoping she could see a license plate or get her cell phone camera to work.

"The plate was kind of obscured because of the bikes on the back of the truck. I couldn't get my camera to work, and I couldn't go follow them because of the long line of customers waiting."

That night, Tracy told her husband about the sighting. He was supportive, and she decided she would report her experience.

"I searched on the Internet for the family and went to their official website (www.mcstayfamily.org). On their homepage is a link to report sightings. I reported what I saw and left my phone numbers asking them to call me."

No one ever did.

"After a couple of days, I posted some of my experiences on the McStay Facebook page, asking why no one had ever contacted me. I was criticized by many on the page for not dropping everything I was doing to follow the family, even if it meant losing my job. I figured that no one really cared and just dropped it. Until Rick Baker contacted me."

I read Tracy's post on the Facebook page and the hurtful, selfish comments that followed. I wanted to talk to Tracy, so I headed to Southport.

We sat down and talked about that day. Her memory of events was extensive.

The fact is most sightings don't pan out. While the witness sincerely believes that they have seen a missing person, most of the time, they didn't.

Tracy's account was different. This was not a passing glance as most of the McStay sightings have been.

She had engaged the man in conversation and spent close to ten minutes with the woman and the children. She was close to all four, within five feet. Her observations were clear of what they were wearing, the younger child's odd haircut that covered the forehead, the woman's soft-spoken voice, the man's necklace, the hats, the woman's sunglasses, etc.

Regardless of how extensive her contact was with this family, without a picture or video of the family, this would be another dead end.

Tracy had told me that many people stop at her diner to order takeout before or after they take the ferry to Wilmington. The ferry has surveillance cameras, so I headed over to talk to security at the Southport ferry office.

I approached the security department at the office and told them I was writing a book about a missing family from Southern California. One of the ladies then said, "You mean the McStays from Fallbrook?" Everywhere I traveled researching for this book, so many knew about the McStays. Some had followed the mystery from the beginning, and some just knew their names. Either way, everyone cared about the wellbeing of this family, especially the children.

They gave me the contact information for the director of security, whose office is in Morehead City, North Carolina.

Robert "Bobby" Hill is the director of security for the North Carolina Ferry Division, the nation's

second-largest ferry system. His ferries transport approximately one million vehicles and more than 2.1 million passengers each year. He is the division's homeland security officer/coordinator and had recently received the TSA's 2011 Field Honorary Partnership.

I called and talked to Mr. Hill, explaining that the McStays might have traveled on one of his ferries on August 28. He said he would gladly go back and look at the tapes if I would send him some pictures and other information about the McStays. I asked him if I could watch the tapes with him, and he agreed.

We set the appointment for Monday, October 22, at 10:00 a.m.

I arrived at the North Carolina Port Headquarters on Monday at 9:30 a.m. and was escorted to Mr. Hill's office. The security at the port was certainly more than I had expected. Someone always had an eye on me. Refreshing, actually.

Earlier that morning, Mr. Hill had reviewed the tapes from August 28, 9:30 a.m. through 10:45 a.m. He wanted to make sure he actually had archives going back that far.

"I saw the family you are talking about," said Hill as he was booting up his computer so we could look at the video together. "A family of four, much like Tracy described."

When his computer was ready to view the video, he typed in "August 28, 9:30 a.m.–10:45 a.m."

What appeared on his monitor was a surprise.

The surveillance video was a nighttime shot. The lights in the ferry lobby were on, and it was dark outside. The parking lot where the family's gray Toyota Tundra was parked was also dark. This was a video of nine thirty at night, not nine thirty in the morning.

Mr. Hill was shocked. He had just watched the video not two hours earlier.

Not deterred and used to this twilight zone stuff, I asked him if he had a video of the ferry's destination at Fort Fisher in Wilmington. He said he did and logged on to that set of surveillance tapes.

If the ferry left Southport on the ten fifteen boat, it would have arrived at Fort Fisher at 11:00 a.m. So he typed in "10:50 a.m. through 1:00 p.m., August 28, 2012."

Again, only nighttime shots.

Still, there was one more chance to get a look at the family he viewed earlier that morning. I asked him to try and retrieve the files from his cache. While the tapes had "malfunctioned," the cache might still have the images he had viewed. It would be Thursday, October 25, before his admin was back in town to view the cache.

On Thursday, nothing.

We can take many positives away from this experience. First, Tracy's description of the family was accurate. According to Mr. Hill, the man had a "funky hat and looked like a surfer." Summer had a "floppy hat and a hippie skirt." The children had "longer hair," and he couldn't tell if "the younger one was a boy or girl." The truck was indeed a Toyota Tundra with bikes on a rear-mounted bike rack.

So the family that Tracy served in her diner was the same family who took the ferry. We had guessed right.

Was the family the McStays? We will probably never know, but hopefully, recounting this sighting will encourage all to report any possible sighting to the authorities. It is a simple process. Someone may have seen the McStays and, for whatever reason, failed to report it.

Epilogue

So, now, after examining hundreds of pages of emails, financial records, receipts and other documents, we are still left with a number of unanswered questions:

Who was transferring the money from Joseph's accounts and why?

Who had his passwords and were any of Joseph's emails tampered with before law enforcement obtained the computer?

Where did the $81,000 from the Saudi fountain go and who took Joseph's receivables?

What did Mike do when he had Joseph's computer for all those days before law enforcement had examined the hard drives? We know he had access to all of Joseph's passwords, and therefore, all his funds.

Most importantly, where are the McStays?

While law enforcement may have believed in the beginning that the family left voluntarily, I think that today they see this case as a murder investigation.

Many who have followed this mystery from the beginning are misinformed in that they believe that if this was an actual murder investigation law enforcement would declare it, and because they have not, it must still be a missing persons case.

Law enforcement is under no obligation to tell the public, or the family for that matter, anything about the case.

Nor are they under any obligation to tell the truth in any way. In fact, we already know they have not been honest when they stated that there had been "no activity on Joseph's bank accounts." We have seen the numerous money-grabbing transfers and attempts to transfer from his Wells Fargo, Union Bank and Bank of America accounts, all the way through July of 2010.

I believe that law enforcement is quietly and patiently biding their time, waiting for someone to slip up. Without a body, there is not much else they can do.

I hope I am wrong. I hope it was the McStays that ordered take-out at a Southport, North Carolina, diner in the fall of 2012.

There are four possibilities. Based on the odds presented from the evidence we do have, let's look at all four:

Summer killed Joseph. Cloudiest background. Not liked by many. Obvious bad judgment. Rubbed almost all who she came in contact with wrong at some point. We have to concede she's capable.

Joseph killed Summer. Did he uncover an affair? Summer's existence got in the way of relationships with Joseph's family, business, friends—you name it. Few would shed tears if she goes. Considering the gravity of what we're dealing with, we can't just write off the most obvious motivations in the whole thing.

The family voluntarily left. A bad business deal, a CPS investigation, an angry loan mod customer? Who knows, but it makes no sense that Joseph would leave that much cash in his accounts.

All four are dead. Why would anyone murder an entire family with two small children? Over a bad fountain deal? Not likely.

I have tried to consider all sides equally throughout these pages, yet most of the time, when the evidence is clear, it all points back to Summer or Mike.

In Summer's history as we have learned it, how long do you think she could stay *anywhere* without ruffling feathers and incurring someone's wrath? Are we to believe that today she earns a living (something she never did a great job of before), makes friends with everybody to keep her secret, and flies happily under the radar with the world looking for her? Where did she suddenly acquire that discipline?

Mike's history in this case reveals a half-brother who has had a difficult time telling the same story twice. And of course, there are the nagging questions such as why it took him 11 days to contact authorities if he was so close to Joseph and what his involvement is with the missing tens of thousands of dollars of Joseph's money.

While these are critical questions, I suppose the one question I ponder more than any other is, how are the boys?

For me, this case has always been about two innocent little boys who were forced to live out the consequences of their parents' poor decisions in life.

Not much different from many of us, I suppose, but they were innocent nonetheless.

Gianni and Joseph Mateo may never completely understand why their lives changed so drastically on the night of February 4, 2010. Hopefully, wherever they are today, they don't care because they are loved and cherished by both parents, if they are still together and still alive.

Do you have a different scenario for what happened to the family? If so, I would like to hear it. Post your theory at www.rickgbaker.blogspot.com and continue to follow my page for updates on this mystery, including the sequel to this book.

My foundation has also offered a $25,000 cash reward for the family, as individuals or as a whole. Go to my blog for details.

Review Board Responds To Patrick McStay

From the beginning of the disappearance, Patrick McStay has complained that law enforcement has made many mistakes in this case, from failing to provide him timely updates to prematurely releasing a suspect in the case. He filed an official complaint with the County of San Diego Citizens' Law Enforcement Review Board and here are their findings in a report dated May 16, 2012:

NO. 11-031

1. Misconduct/Procedure – Deputy 2 "miscategorized" a missing family for 11 months before acknowledging that "something bad happened."

    Board Finding: Action Justified

    Rationale: The complainant believed that the case was not properly classified to ensure proper investigation. The case was classified as a Missing Persons case since it was initially reported on February 15, 2010. Because of the unknown circumstances surrounding the missing persons, Homicide Detective Deputy 2 was assigned to investigate the disappearance in accordance with Sheriff's Department Policy 6.57, Missing Persons. There has been no evidence uncovered to show that a crime has been committed to warrant another classification. Deputy 2 acknowledged that he offered his opinion to the family and the media after eleven months stating that "something bad had happened," or words to that effect, because the missing family's disappearance had not been solved. The Missing Persons case remains open and active and will remain so until the family is located or evidence of a crime is determined. The evidence shows that the case has been properly classified as Missing Persons was lawful, justified, and proper.

2. Misconduct/Procedure – Deputies 2 and 3 withheld information from the complainant during an ongoing investigation.

    Board Finding: Action Justified

    Rationale: The complainant stated that he shared with Deputy 2 information/evidence that he discovered, and Deputies 2 and 3 failed to provide any update or status reports regarding that information/evidence; nor did they provide any reciprocal information. Deputy 2 stated that he shared information with the complainant that was available to other family members provided it did not damage the integrity of the investigation. Deputy 3 declined to respond to the complainant's request for information in order to preserve the integrity of the investigation. Department Policy 7.3, Release of Information, precludes release of any information pertaining to cases under investigation. The evidence shows the alleged conduct did lawful, occur but was justified and proper.

3. Misconduct/Procedure – Deputy 2 failed to respond to the complainant's email and telephone contacts.

    Board Finding: Action Justified

    Rationale: Deputy 2 and the complainant communicated on occasion via email and telephone until early February 2011. During the period February 6-10, 2011 the complainant sent Deputy 2 a number of emails offering information and opinions related to events and evidence that he discovered. The complainant was insistent in his communications and challenged the credibility and integrity of the Missing Persons investigation. Deputy 2 was advised by his supervisor, Deputy 3, to no longer communicate with the complainant. Deputy 3 notified the complainant via e-mail that all communications with San Diego Sheriff's Department should now be directed to Deputy 3. Deputy 2 complied with the direction of his supervisor and the evidence shows the alleged conduct did occur but was lawful, justified and proper.

4. Misconduct/Procedure – Deputy 3 used "poor communication and management skills" during his contact(s) with the complainant.

   Board Finding: Unfounded

   Rationale: Deputy 3 contacted the complainant after the complainant was unsuccessful in contacting Deputy 2 during the period February 6-10, 2011. Deputy 3, Deputy 2's supervisor, advised the complainant that he had been monitoring the case, was satisfied that the investigation had been thorough, and acknowledged that the investigation continued in search of his missing family members. Deputy 3 additionally offered to accept communications from the complainant regarding the investigation. The complainant believed that Deputy 3's intervention was intended to threaten and intimidate him, and indicated that he would refrain from future communication. Deputy 3's email communications were accomplished professionally and there was no evidence to show poor communication and management skills. The evidence shows that the alleged act did not occur.

5. Misconduct/Harassment – Deputy 1 sent the complainant e-mails intended for internal staff.

   Board Finding: Unfounded

   Rationale: Deputy 1 did include the complainant on one e-mail with multiple addressees which conveyed his opinion that

Deputy 3 had adequately responded to the complainant's concerns. There was no evidence to demonstrate that Deputy 1 intended to harass the complainant. The evidence shows that the alleged harassment did not occur.

6. Misconduct/Harassment –Deputy 4 sent the complainant e-mails intended for internal staff.

Board Finding: Summary Dismissal

Rationale: Deputy 4 retired from the San Diego Sheriff's Department in May 2011 and is no longer employed by San Diego County Sheriff's Department. The Review Board lacks jurisdiction.

7. Misconduct/Procedure – Deputy 2 prematurely dismissed a suspect in an ongoing investigation without conducting a proper investigation.

Board Finding: Not Sustained

Rationale: The complainant provided investigators with information about individuals he believed warranted investigation. Deputy 2 stated that all leads, provided by the complainant or any other source, were pursued in a timely manner. Deputy 2 interviewed all persons believed to hold pertinent information related to the disappearance of the Missing Persons. The Missing Persons case remains active and open and complete investigative documents were not available for review. Without access to the complete investigation there was insufficient evidence to either prove or disprove the allegation.

8. Misconduct/Procedure – Deputy 2, as the detective of record, failed to ensure accurate information on the FBI and/or Interpol websites.

Board Finding: Not Sustained

Rationale: The complainant contacted Deputy 2 in October 2010 and stated that the Missing Persons information was not available on Federal Bureau of Investigation or Interpol websites. The initial Missing Persons Report identifying all four missing persons and a Be-on-Lookout broadcast were completed by the responding patrol deputy on February 15, 2010, as required by Department Policy and Procedure 6.57. These reports facilitated rapid entry into the Missing/Unidentified Persons System. Deputy 2 stated that he submitted Information to Interpol on February 23, 2010. As a result of communications between the complainant and Deputy 2 in October 2010 Deputy 2 learned that one of the missing children did not appear on the Interpol public website. Deputy 2 contacted Interpol and was advised that the law enforcement site was accurate and they would ensure the public site was corrected. All four missing persons now appear on the FBI and Interpol websites available to the public. The Missing Persons case remains active and open and complete investigative documents were not available for review. Without access to the complete investigation there was insufficient evidence to either prove or disprove the allegation.

9. Misconduct/Procedure – Deputy 2 "confirmed" that video of family crossing San Ysidro Border Crossing was a family reportedly missing.

Board Finding: Not Sustained

Rationale: The complainant stated that Deputy 2 confirmed in many media reports that the family seen at the San Ysidro Border Crossing was the missing family. Deputy 2 denied stating that he confirmed the family seen crossing the San Ysidro Border Crossing were the subjects of the Missing Persons Investigation. He has publicly stated on many occasions that based on the evidence of the case, combined with surveillance video, that he believed the family seen crossing the San Ysidro Border was likely to be but would not positively confirm that they were the subjects of the Missing Persons Investigation. Deputy 2 has commented on the San Ysidro Border Crossing video in hundreds of media interviews, as such there was insufficient evidence to either prove or disprove the allegation.

10. Misconduct/Procedure – Deputy 2, failed to search, in a timely fashion, the electronic files of a missing family.

Board Finding: Not Sustained

Rationale: The complainant stated that Deputy 2 failed to search and read every electronic file stored on the family computers. Deputy 2 used approved department protocol by having the San Diego FBI Regional Forensic Computer Laboratory analyze many thousands of files on the family computers; a process which the complainant felt was insufficient. Deputy 2 stated that analysis was received approximately 30 days after requested and this information was utilized in the conduct of the Missing Persons investigation. The Missing Persons case remains active and open and complete investigative documents were not available for review. Without access to the complete investigation there was insufficient evidence to either prove or disprove the allegation.

11. Misconduct/Procedure – Deputy 2, failed to investigate a person of interest.

Board Finding: Not Sustained

Rationale: The complainant stated that investigators had failed to investigate an individual he believed to be a person of interest. Deputy 2 stated that all leads, provided by the complainant or any other source, were pursued in a timely manner. Deputy 2 interviewed all persons believed to hold pertinent information related to the disappearance of the Missing Persons. The Missing Persons case remains active and open and complete investigative documents were not available for review. Without access to the complete investigation there was insufficient evidence to either prove or disprove the allegation.

12. Misconduct/Procedure – Deputy 2 failed to investigate family financial transactions in a timely manner.

Board Finding: Not Sustained

Rationale: The complainant believed that Deputy 2 had not conducted a thorough and timely review of family financial transactions. Deputy 2 denied that he failed to investigate family financial transactions in a timely manner. The Missing Persons case remains active and open and complete investigative documents were not available for review. Without access to the complete investigation there was insufficient evidence to either prove or disprove the allegation.

Law Enforcement Quotes

Detective Troy Dugal, San Diego Sheriff's Department

It is important to remember that when law enforcement speaks to media or the general public, they may not be telling the truth. Often times the quotes they give may not be directed to the public at all, but to a suspect or others connected to a case.

Regarding these quotes from Detective Dugal, keep in mind two things: First, unless we hear the exact quote from the detective himself, as in the America's Most Wanted piece from June 2010, we cannot be certain he was quoted correctly by the media. And second, the quote may have been directed to specific individuals in this case such as an unnamed suspect or the family itself.

June, 2010

"I hope it's voluntary missing but I have to believe it's worse than that."

America's Most Wanted, June, 2010.

December 24, 2010

"I can't prove that they left of their own accord,"
investigator DuGal said. "If I could, this case
would be closed. But because there is a small
possibility that there is foul play involved, it
remains open.

"There is no indication that they were running
away from something. I try to keep my mind
open to foul play, but also to prove if they left
on their own. I can't get a hit either way."

http://www.nctimes.com/mobile/
articl...018576103.html

January 6, 2011

"From the initial investigation, our biggest
fear was that the family had been abducted.
We obtained a search warrant to either
substantiate or alleviate that concern with
physical evidence.

"Now, we know that they were not abducted
in a vehicle, or physically abducted, but that
does not rule out verbal abduction, in which
someone told them they needed to be somewhere,
fast."

"There is no trail supporting evidence of
foul play. Telephone calls within a month of

the McStays' disappearance have all been identified. In summary, calls had been made to family members, business partners, and hair salons. Du Gal said none of the individuals he has interviewed that had been speaking to the McStay's made him suspicious."

"We have looked at financial records, Summer's bank accounts, Joseph and Summer's joint account, and Joseph's business account," said DuGal, who also said email and cell phone accounts have been completely inactive since the family's disappearance. "All the accounts have been red-flagged and none of them have been touched since February 4. Prior to the family going missing, the account's activity had been normal. There had been no major withdrawals or [an indication that they were] putting money under a pillow for a vacation."

"When the finances were frozen, the 'auto-pay' on the mortgage also stopped. It is protocol to freeze the account of missing persons."

"We get some very vague tips, such as people saying they think they saw a family that resembled the McStays two to ten days ago at a certain location. To put that tip to rest, I have to hope the business has 24-hour video footage and then review 10 days' worth of footage. Even then, it's just impossible to work with *that because the family could have been seen 11 or 12 days ago, as opposed to the 10 days ago."*

"Since I started working in homicide two years ago, no other case has taken up more time than this one. This case has taken more time and man-hours than any other in my career. I also have three direct partners who I have tasked with interviews and investigating other search warrants. They have spent a considerable amount of time investigating the case. Outside of the Sheriff's office, the FBI and Department of Justice have become invested, as have Immigration and Customs and the Mexican Federal Police. There is no simple way to answer how many man-hours have been spent on this case."

"That's the mystery," explained DuGal. "In my whole career, I have never seen anything like this. Usually when something bad happens, there's a trail left behind. There is a witness or someone who has come forward. If the family had picked up and left Fallbrook, there would also be signs. But the case remains between both extremes, with neither side satisfied."

"This missing persons case is open and active, and will remain mine for as long as my career exists or until we find the family. It wouldn't make sense for this case to become a cold case, and it will remain so until we have found

the location of the entire family. All four must be found, and we are still hoping for a good outcome."

"If we are going to believe that the family crossed the international border on Feb. 8, we have to think that it is probable that someone saw the McStays before they crossed," said DuGal. "We know for a fact that their vehicle did not cross the border, and that the family did not use their credit cards, cell phone, or accounts. After checking multiple times with various agencies, we are also 100 percent certain that the family is not in protective custody. So, where are they?"

http://www.thevillagenews.com/story/53576/

February 4, 2011

"I am confident the McStays have not traveled out of Mexico unless they are using an assumed name."

http://www.hispanicallyspeakingnews....-the-run/4981/

February 6, 2011

"Something very good, or something very bad happened within that house among the four people there."

"I believe something occurred within those four walls between the four family members that made them leave in a hurry. It may have been good. It may have been bad. I don't know."

"I absolutely know their financials and their friends better than I know my own financials and my wife's friends."

http://www.msnbc.msn.com/id/41448084.../#. UKG6T4awUzQ

February 10, 2011

"I absolutely know their financials and their friends better than I know my own financials and my wife's friends."

"I think it's likely that something bad has happened."

"Summer did not care for her Hispanic heritage," DuGal said. "Therefore, she assumed identities in the things she liked."

"I believe something occurred within those four walls between the four family members that made them leave in a hurry. It may have been good. It may have been bad. I don't know."

"We're a year into this. I want to find the family."

http://www.legalnews.com/detroit/871708

May 30, 2011

"It looked like somebody left in a hurry," he [Dugal] recalled. "Not frantically, but in a hurry."

"The bottom line was that life was normal for the McStays up to Feb. 4, and on that day they just vanished. And after that day, neither Summer nor Joseph existed on paper."

"A week before the family disappeared, someone used the desktop computer to research travel to Mexico. One search specifically asked: 'What documents do children need for traveling to Mexico?'"

http://articles.latimes.com/2011/may... amily-20110530

Following The Money Trail

February 8,9: Someone ordered a copy of Joseph's Quickbooks accounting program four days after the disappearance and before they were reported missing.

Bank Account Transfer Complete

service@paypal.com   Add to contacts
To Earth Inspired Products

2/09/10
Reply

Hello Earth Inspired Products,

You added $2,000.00 USD to your PayPal balance from your bank account. Your money is now available in your PayPal account.

Thanks,

PayPal

February 9: Someone transferred $2,000 from
Joseph's bank account into his PayPal account.

Bank Account Transfer Complete

2/09/10

To Earth Inspired Products
From: service@paypal.com (service@paypal.com)
Sent: Tue 2/09/10 8:21 AM
To: Earth Inspired Products (josephmcstay69@hotmail.com)

Hello Earth Inspired Products,

You added $2,000.00 USD to your PayPal balance from your bank account. Your money is now available in your PayPal account.

Thanks,

PayPal

Wells Fargo Contact Information Updated

Wells Fargo Online   Add to contacts
To josephmcstay69@hotmail.com

2/12/10
Reply

wellsfargo.com

Your contact information has been updated
We have updated your Wells Fargo contact information:

• Mailing Address

To view the updates, or make additional updates, sign on to update your contact information

If you did not make this request online, by phone, or at a Wells Fargo branch, please call us immediately at 1-800-869-3557 (for personal banking) or 1-800-225-5935 (for small business banking). We are available 24 hours a day, 7 days a week. Please do not reply to this email.

Note: If you use Bill Pay, you will need to update your contact information for that service separately. You'll find a link on the right side of the Update Your Contact Information screen.

wellsfargo.com | Fraud Information Center

February 12: Someone changed the mailing address
on Joseph's Wells Fargo business account.

February 18: Someone transfers $3,000 into Dan Kavanaugh's account.

February 18: Someone transferred $2,000 from Joseph's bank account into his PayPal account.

February 24: Someone transfers $2,000 from Joseph's PayPal account into Dan Kavanaugh's account.

March 4: Someone initiates a transfer from Joseph's
business account into his PayPal account.

March 9: Someone transfers $2,900 from
Joseph's bank account into his PayPal account.

March 11: Someone transfers $3,000 from Joseph's
PayPal account into Dan Kavanaugh's account.

March 16: Mike McStay registers
EarthInspiredProducts.com. Joseph' company
was registered as Earth Inspired Products.

March 25: Someone transfers $3,445 from Joseph's
PayPal account into Dan Kavanaugh's account.

March 25: Someone transfers $5,000 from Joseph's
PayPal account into Mike McStay's account.

May 5: Someone tries to transfer money from Joseph's
Union Bank account into his PayPal account.

June 1: Someone tries to transfer money from
Joseph's Bank account into his PayPal account.

Electronic funds transfer declined

Hello Earth Inspired Products,

You recently tried to refund a payment by transferring funds from your bank account to your PayPal account.

Union Bank of California declined your funds transfer.

Because your transfer was declined, this refund has been canceled.

Thanks,

PayPal

June 1: Someone tries to transfer money from Joseph's
Union Bank account into his PayPal account.

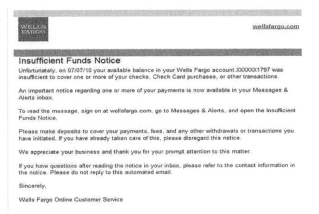

Electronic funds transfer declined

u service@paypal.com Add to contacts
To Earth Inspired Products

Hello Earth Inspired Products,

You recently tried to transfer funds from your Bank of America bank account.

Bank of America declined your funds transfer.

Because Bank of America declined your transfer, this transaction has been canceled.

Thanks,

PayPal

PROTECT YOUR PASSWORD

NEVER give your password to anyone, including PayPal employees. Protect yourself against fraudulent websites by opening a new web browser (e.g. Internet Explorer or Firefox) and typing in the PayPal URL every time you log in to your account.

June 7: Someone tries to transfer money from Joseph's Bank of America account into his PayPal account.

WELLS FARGO   wellsfargo.com

Insufficient Funds Notice

Unfortunately, on 07/07/10 your available balance in your Wells Fargo account XXXXXX1797 was insufficient to cover one or more of your checks, Check Card purchases, or other transactions.

An important notice regarding one or more of your payments is now available in your Messages & Alerts inbox.

To read the message, sign on at wellsfargo.com, go to Messages & Alerts, and open the Insufficient Funds Notice.

Please make deposits to cover your payments, fees, and any other withdrawals or transactions you have initiated. If you have already taken care of this, please disregard this notice.

We appreciate your business and thank you for your prompt attention to this matter.

If you have questions after reading the notice in your inbox, please refer to the contact information in the notice. Please do not reply to this automated email.

Sincerely,

Wells Fargo Online Customer Service

July 7: Joseph's Wells Fargo Bank account is overdrawn.

July 16: PayPal refunds one of Joseph's clients $1,500.

July 20: Is this a new Capital One credit
card in Joseph's name or an old one
sent with new expiration date?

CPSIA information can be obtained at www.ICGtesting.com
Printed in the USA
LVOW02s1423091213

364544LV00008B/67/P

9 781625 104212